The Search For The Pale Prophet In Ancient America

By Sean Casteel

Introduction By Timothy Green Beckley

The Search For
The Pale Prophet
In Ancient America
by
Sean Casteel
With an Introduction by Timothy Green Beckley

This edition Copyright © 2015 by Global Communications/Conspiracy Journal

All rights reserved. No part of these manuscripts may be copied or reproduced by any mechanical or digital methods and no exerpts or quotes may be used in any other book or manuscript without permission in writing by the Publisher, Global Communications/Conspiracy Journal, except by a reviewer who may quote brief passages in a review.

Revised Edition

Published in the United States of America By
Global Communications/Conspiracy Journal
Box 753 · New Brunswick, NJ 08903

Staff Members
Timothy G. Beckley, Publisher
Carol Ann Rodriguez, Assistant to the Publisher
Sean Casteel, General Associate Editor
Tim R. Swartz, Graphics and Editorial Consultant
William Kern, Editorial and Art Consultant

Sign Up On The Web For Our Free Weekly Newsletter
and Mail Order Version of Conspiracy Journal
and Bizarre Bazaar
www.ConspiracyJournal.com

Order Hot Line: 1-732-602-3407
PayPal: MrUFO8@hotmail.com

Introduction by Timothy Green Beckley xi

SECTION ONE, THE STORY OF TAYLOR HANSEN AND THE PALE PROPHET
1. A Brief Biography of L. Taylor Hansen
   The Sci-Fi Feminist Disguised as a Man 3
2. An Introductory Overview of "He Walked The Americas" 7
3. The Man/Woman Scholar Is Charged With A Mission 15
4. Polynesia: The Prophet's Journey Begins 17
5. Peru, Brazil and Guatemala: The Mission of Mercy Continues 21
6. The Heartless Queen of the Yucatan 27
7. The Future, a Lost Fawn and the Prophet's Birth 31
8. The Angry Prophet Among the Pawnee 35
9. Teaching the Ways of Peace 39
10. The Truth of the Pale God Is Preserved 43
11. The Pale Prophet Strikes Water and Hansen Speaks to the Snake Priest 49
12. An Assassination Attempt on the Messenger of Peace 55
13. The Master's Authority 57
14. The Pale Prophet Departs the Americas 59
15. Just Who Was The Prophet? 61

SECTION TWO, SELECTED ESSAYS FROM "AMAZING STORIES"
16. The White Race—Does It Exist? 67
17. The Bearded White Prophet 71
18. The Totem Of The Wolf 77
19. The Mystery Of Apache Tradition 83
20. Tribal Memories Of The Flying Saucers 95
21. Where Was The War Of The Wind God? 101
22. Totem Of The Fish 107
23. More Shadows Of Ancient India 115
24. The Ghost Of The Venus Calendar 121

SEAN CASTEEL

Sean Casteel has written about UFOs, alien abduction, and related phenomena since 1989 when he interviewed Whitley Strieber, around the time that the movie version of "Communion" was released. He was a contributor for several years to UFO UNIVERSE and was eventually given the title of Associate Editor. Later he began to write special reports and books for both of Tim Beckley's publishing companies, Inner Light Publications and Global Communications. The books he has written include "UFOs, Prophecy and the End of Time," "The Heretic's UFO Guidebook" and "Signs and Symbols of the Second Coming." His work has also been published in the U.K., Italy, Romania and Australia.

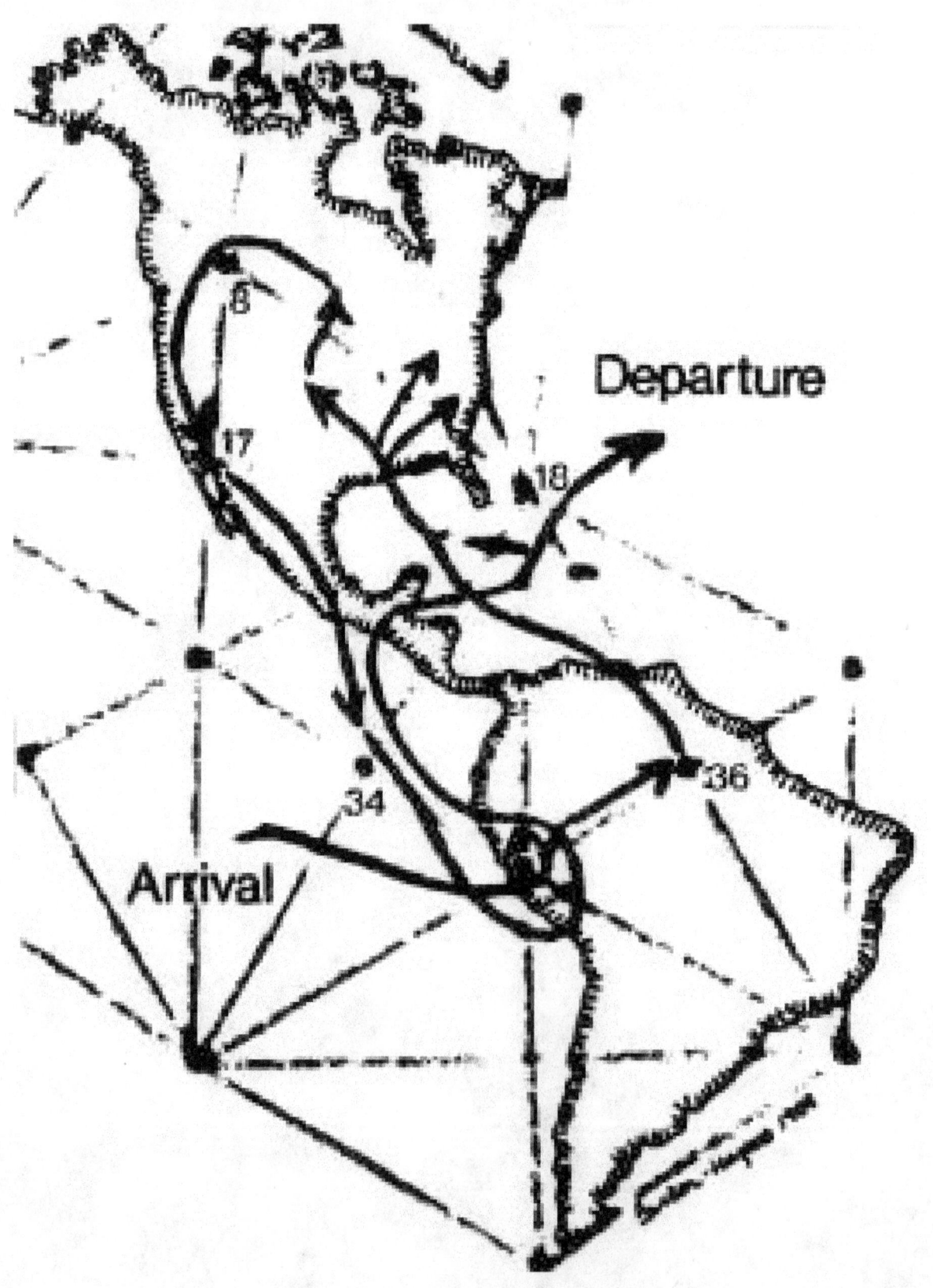

The Prophet Raises a Giant Rock

Publisher Tim Beckley stands before Native American mural at Coffee Pot in Sedona, AZ. (Photo by Charla Gené)

A NOTE ABOUT THE LINE ILLUSTRATIONS USED IN THIS BOOK

The illustrations used to depict various myths, legends and rituals in this book were scanned from printed copies of "Amazing Stories" pulp magazine from the years of 1939 to 1971. They were scanned by an unknown source to a size approximately that of a business card at a very low resolution. They have been enhanced where possible with little success. The publisher feels it is better to include the illustrations so readers can see for themselves the types of essays L. Taylor Hansen was writing during those years.
—The Publisher

Introduction

THE MYSTERIOUS "PALE PROPHET" WHO WALKED THE AMERICAS AND THE LIFE OF L. TAYLOR HANSEN

By Timothy Green Beckley, Publisher/Editor-In-Chief

L. Taylor Hansen is one of the most remarkable writers/researchers on a most remarkable topic.

After reading her volume, **He Walked The Americas** (Amherst Press), and studying what we might term "fringe archeology," it becomes apparent that no one group can be credited with "discovering" the Americas. Not Christopher Columbus! Leif Eriksson! The Chinese! Not even the Knights Templar! Or Francis Bacon!

Yep, 1492 may be a date underlined in bold in our school books, but the truth of the matter could be much different than we have been told.

It could be – and seems most likely – that explorers from various countries and continents were passing each other as they crossed the oceans back and forth to what ultimately became known as the Americas – North and South. Though these explorers may not have set up settlements early on, at least one individual approximately two thousand years ago walked among the tribes.

These are the legends of the Healer. From the Polynesian Islands to the eastern seaboard of the United States, from Canada to South America, they called him by different names - the Healer, the Prophet, the Miracle Worker, God of the Dawn Light, the Wind God, the Teacher, the White-Robed Master.

But, really, who was this "Pale Prophet" said to be a remarkable healer and who spoke the many languages of the various native tribes he is said to have visited? Through a series of "unusual circumstances," Ms. Taylor (she definitely was NOT a man, as most readers assumed from the structure of her unisex name) gives us the impression that this individual might have been Jesus of Nazareth on a walkabout, spreading his love and compassion far and wide throughout the unestablished world, as we shall see from Sean Casteel's expanded investigation of the intriguing possibilities that we are now confronted with.

Those who have critiqued this volume with its elaborate layout and glossy paper have taken various positions as to the stories told by L. Taylor Hansen, which she based on spoken-word narratives related to her by various shamans and chieftains in her fieldwork. One of her biggest supporters would be the Mormon Church, who have, since the very beginning of their movement by Joseph Smith, included such accounts of a messiah-like individual (or individuals) parting the thick foliage of the landscape and commanding the attention of those living there in their aboriginal settlements. Others of a more skeptical bent believe that if there was any truth to these various accounts that mainstream anthropologists would have long ago confirmed such visitations.

Hogwash! There is so much that we do not know about the history of the world because it has been kept from us by those academics who have an agenda in mind when they censor the facts from truth seekers like you and I.

As an example of what has been noted by those that ponder such perplexities, I quote the following mini-review of Hansen's hard-backed volume **He Walked The Americas** that I found posted on the Internet: *"I am not sure how the author was able to figure out the order in which this person traveled through the Americas. However, that being beside the point, what is fascinating is that there are so many legends and stories of a person who walked the Americas. Someone who could heal and teach and believed in peace and love. The similarities to Christ are fascinating. Particularly when you consider the Book of Mormon, another testament of Christ, indicates that yes, Christ did walk and teach the people who lived here. Even more amazing is that these stories in this book are only the tip of the iceberg so to speak. Many of the stories refer to other stories that are about this man who walked and taught over here. It is my understanding that there are stories among the Indians of floods that covered the Earth and other stories that are similar to the Bible stories. So this really shouldn't be such a big surprise. This is one book I'm not sorry I bought and read.*

But enough said about **He Walked The Americas**, except that those who want to do a follow up should go to Amazon.com and order a copy of this remarkable volume or through the mail directly from the son of the late Raymond A. Palmer, the original publisher. Raymond B. Palmer has kept this massively important book in print and offers it at a very reasonable price with all its color plates and semi-slick composition. He still resides in Amherst, Wisconsin, just like his late father. Several years back, I was privileged to be part of a panel that interviewed the man whose father gave life to such topics as flying saucers, the hollow earth, and another important book, **Oahspe**.

This particular episode of www.TheParacast.com, recorded on January 13, 2013, can easily be found on the web by using your favorite search engine.

But I do not want to give readers the false impression that the work that you are now starting to read is totally about the matter of the "Pale Prophet" who traveled the vast expanse of the Americas. And, furthermore, how could he have accomplished this feat since the territory he visited would have taken up thousands and thousands of miles? Impossible to walk, certainly, while a lot of places he could not have arrived by boat. UFO? Well, anything is almost possible.

For you see the subject of our inquiry, L. Taylor Hansen, was a very inquisitive individual. **She** (I repeat her gender again for those who might have glossed over it the first time the subject was mentioned). The reason she adopted this masculine derivative of her actual name was because she was determined to break into the all-male-dominated circle of science fiction and pulp magazine writers where she knew it would be almost impossible to be accepted because of her being a member of the distaff sex.

For all intents and purposes, we can call her the first feminist of science fiction, though her writing was as hard-hitting as that of any testosterone-laden journalist who wrote about battling Martians and zipping off to the far flung reaches of the galaxy only to be molested by some tentacle-bearing monster.

You can check out some of the rather provocative covers of the magazines she wrote for to get the gist of what I am referring to.

This work by Mr. Casteel covers a remarkable range of topics, all interrelated, from the "Pale Prophet" to the travels worldwide of an individual some have thought of as the Christ. I, myself, am not sold on this concept, but it is an interesting idea that the faithful may find possible to hold close to their heart. We also are reprinting a selection of essays Hansen wrote that appeared in her column for "Amazing Stories," called "Scientific Mysteries," for several years back in the 1940s.

Overall, this book offers a window into the past that we can look through to better understand the development of extra-Biblical approaches to Christ and the hold such mysteries still have on our beliefs.

Tim Beckley, NY, NY
MrUFO8@hotmail.com
www.ConspiracyJournal.Com

YouTube Channel – Mr. UFOs Secret Files
Weekly Podcast "Exploring The Bizarre" – KCOR.Com

Part One

The story of L. Taylor Hansen and her search for the Pale Prophet who walked the Americas. With Biblical insights and interpretations not present in the original text added by author Sean Casteel.

THE SEARCH FOR THE "PALE PROPHET" IN ANCIENT AMERICA

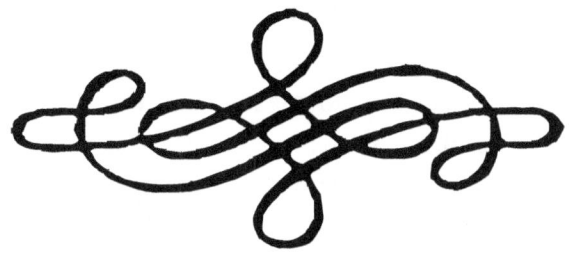

A Brief Biography of L. Taylor Hansen
The Sci-Fi Feminist Disguised as a Man

Born in 1897, L. Taylor Hansen was a popular science writer who would come to pen a popular and much-referred-to text on the idea that Jesus Christ visited the Americas in the first century A.D. to deliver a message of love and peace to the indigenous peoples there. The initial "L" in Hansen's name stood for "Lucile," which was a fact she would keep hidden for many years. In her early years, as she made a name for herself as a writer, she disguised herself as a man in order to have her work taken more seriously in the male-dominated world of anthropology.

Hansen is the author of eight science fiction short stories, nearly sixty nonfiction articles popularizing anthropology and geology, and three nonfiction books, including "He Walked The Americas," her book on a mysterious prophet and healer who journeyed among the natives of North, Central and South America.

While little is known about Hansen, most likely because she preferred to keep herself – and even her gender – hidden from her own reading public, she did at one time talk of her childhood memories of staying with her parents in an abandoned fort after the "Indian Wars," which had been fought from the time of the earliest colonial settlements of the European whites until the "closing of the frontier" in 1890.

Hansen described her father as a young "West Pointer" who brought his wife and daughter to his first assignment after leaving the academy, a broken down fort from which the U.S. Army had once waged war against the indigenous peoples.

"Could that have been an omen of my later interest?" Hansen would ask in some of her rare autobiographical writings. Her first nurse was a maiden of the Sioux tribe who at one point tossed her down a winding flight of stairs to quiet her crying.

THE SEARCH FOR THE "PALE PROPHET" IN ANCIENT AMERICA

"What the girl did not know," Hansen writes, "is that my father, just entering the front door, had been on the football team at West Point and was adept at catching forward passes. Perhaps that was an omen of a life of travel with overtones of adventure."

In 1919, she writes, she was initiated into the Ojibway (Chippewa) tribe with blood rites because she had suggested to the tribe that "a group of orators be sent to Washington, D.C., to protest the tenure of an agency doctor – who gave them whiskey instead of medicine – rather than just killing the offender."

Hansen was a college student at the time and required to write a paper for one of her classes.

"Since I was about to spend my summer vacation on Lake Superior in Michigan with a group of students," she writes, "the subject of Indian legends seemed an excellent linking of pleasure and duty. It was here that I first heard the Legend of the White Prophet and regarded it with amusement as a garbled memory of early missionary instruction. My teacher agreed."

Hansen said the stories she heard that summer offered her no great knowledge, consisting mainly of "Brer Rabbit"-type tales of talking animals that held little meaning for her. But she did learn that she had a talent for getting into adventurous situations.

Hansen's next contact with Native Americans happened ten years later, after she had a Bachelor's Degree, some business experience, and had done some graduate study in geology and anthropology at the University of California, Los Angeles.

"A great uncle had left me some two thousand dollars," she writes. "My parents, both being dead by now, I shook off all family proposals of various business ventures and took a grand circle tour of the far north."

On that tour, she would eventually travel a thousand miles by dog team. As is so typical of Hansen, she did not hesitate to follow her dream.

"During this never-to-be-forgotten year," she recalled, "I had contact with many tribes and once more the recurring White Prophet legend. I regarded this flood of 'white men' with various names as most confusing, but I was becoming much interested in the migration legends of various tribes."

After her year of living dangerously, Hansen returned to more graduate work in the fields of anthropology and geology and added archeology to that list. It was then that she began to write science fiction to cover her living expenses and began to gain some recognition as an author. But the outlets for her sci-fi stories went under with the arrival of the Great Depression. She fell ill and went to Mexico to recover. There she met Sedillio, Chief of the Yaquis.

"With all due apology to the many brilliant scientists and other learned men

THE SEARCH FOR THE "PALE PROPHET" IN ANCIENT AMERICA

I have worked with and trained under at five universities," she writes, "this red-skinned wild leader of his people was the most learned and the most brilliant. I began to understand the symbolism of the legends and to guess the vastness and magnificence of the 'Serpent Empire,' of whom he was one of the 'Great Suns,' or hereditary leaders."

When Hansen was in her mid-40s, she began to write a regular column called "Scientific Mysteries" in the pulp magazine "Amazing Stories." Although "Amazing Stories" was predominately filled with sci-fi and fantasy stories (Ray Bradbury was a regular contributor), Hansen was given space to air her theories on geology and anthropology in real-world scientific terms.

Her first pieces for "Amazing Stories" concerned the work of her father, Frank Bursley Taylor, regarding continental drift theory. Continental drift is the name given to the supposed movement of the Earth's continents relative to each other, causing the great landmasses to appear to "drift" across the ocean bed. The theory started in the 1500s and gradually drew more proponents. For instance, in 1858, Antonio Snider-Pellegrini postulated that the eastern coast of the Americas was once locked together with the western coast of Africa before some cataclysm separated them to create the Atlantic Ocean. He produced a map showing that the coast lines of the two continents fit together neatly, like pieces of a huge geological puzzle.

In Hansen's time, the most famous proponent of the theory was Germany's Alfred Wegener, who acknowledged the similarity of his ideas to those of Frank Bursley Taylor, which had preceded the German scientist by a few years. The unproved notion of continental drift would lay the foundation for Hansen's later arguments that some of the stories of Native American lore might have origins in common with legends from other far-flung parts of the world, such as Europe, Africa and India. If it could be established that the various continents were initially part of one huge landmass, the fact that they espoused the same religious and historical "mythology" would follow naturally enough.

When Hansen began to tackle anthropology in her columns for "Amazing Stories," she did not shy away from the controversial issues the field was embroiled in. In the years before World War II, the last vestiges of scientific racism were falling away, and Hansen was on the forefront of the movement. She wrote boldly about her belief that the "standards of color are far too superficial."

One prevailing concept she opposed involved the idea that the races differ culturally because of their distinctive skull geometries. She points out that the skull shape of the Mayans does not affect their intelligence. She also contended that Africans are not primitive but in fact more highly evolved than other human types.

In one of her columns for "Amazing Stories," published in their July-August

THE SEARCH FOR THE "PALE PROPHET" IN ANCIENT AMERICA

1942 issue and called "The White Race – Does It Exist?", she begins by writing, "When we speak of the races of the earth, is there really such a thing as the white race? Is the color of a man's skin indicative of his origin? There is no subject upon which more scientific nonsense, or rather let us say nonsense purporting to be science, has been written than upon the subject of race. The reason is not hard to find. Each man prefers his own type and considers his to be the highest. It is a subject which is more bound up with emotion than with reason, and the average man is still an emotional animal."

Hansen goes on to catalog some of the preferences popular in her time, including the German prejudice in favor of white-skinned, Aryan-looking blue-eyed blondes. This was 1942, remember, and Hitler was still in power and waging war against the Allies for the sake of spreading his pro-Aryan philosophy throughout the world.

But Hansen foresaw the inevitable changes that would be wrought in the scientific community, especially among its anthropologists.

"The ideas of race which were popular during the days of our fathers," she writes, "are at present giving place to other standards of differentiation. If the tendency continues to its inevitable conclusion, we are going to discover that there is no such thing as a white race. For the standards of color by which our parents learned to classify mankind are far too superficial for the most advanced anthropologists."

What follows in this book is an analysis of the writings of L. Taylor Hansen as she moves beyond the prejudice and bigotry of her times to arrive at a new way of seeing the equality of mankind as well as a view of Jesus as the "Pale Prophet" who compassionately embraced the so-called "primitive" peoples of the Americas, leaving a mysterious legacy behind that Hansen would spend a great many years recording and coming to understand.

THE SEARCH FOR THE "PALE PROPHET" IN ANCIENT AMERICA

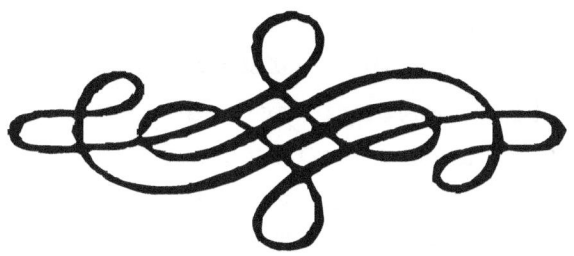

An Introductory Overview of "He Walked The Americas"

L. Taylor Hansen may not be a household name, even among believers in extra-Biblical accounts of Jesus, but she nevertheless has her followers and adherents even in this high-tech 21st century. Although material on Hansen may be scant, one can find online tributes to her work that help to add to an inspiring whole, a more nearly complete account of Jesus and his love for all the peoples of the Earth.

A writer named Bette Stockbauer has made available online an excellent overview of Hansen's classic book, "He Walked The Americas," that serves as a good place to begin our study of Hansen's life and work. To accompany Stockbauer's summary of Hansen's book, I have inserted my own Biblical correlations to the ancient indigenous legends handed down through two millennia.

THE MYSTERIOUS PALE STRANGER ARRIVES

"From the Polynesian Islands to the eastern seaboard of the United States," Stockbauer begins, "from Canada to South America, they called him by different names – the Healer, the Prophet, the Miracle Worker, God of the Dawn Light, the Wind God, the Teacher, the White-Robed Master. Although the names are different, the legends are sung the same.

"In Polynesia, they tell of three great ships that sailed from the West. Moving across the water, there appeared a fair-skinned man in a long white garment, brown hair and beard glowing gold in the morning sun. When He reached the land, people saw that His robe was dry. Thus they knew He was a God. Scholars ascribe this legend to the 1st century A.D."

Stockbauer then goes on to recount the legend of the Toltecs of central Mexico about a prophet with gray-green eyes and golden sandals. With twelve disciples He taught the people His religion of peace. The Mound Builders of North America recorded tales of a great Healer who could raise the dead and heal the sick.

"He walked among the people," Stockbauer writes, "hands raised in blessing. A mysterious cross graced each palm. Such are the stories whispered by the Holy Men and Keepers of the Legends for nearly 2,000 years."

The time element here is very important. Hansen believed that the Native American stories and legends surrounding the mysterious Pale Prophet were not merely confabulated accounts of the story of Jesus as taught by the missionaries, who would not come until nearly 1,500 years later. Given the various historical clues archeologists and anthropologists use to date such things, the chronology of the Pale Prophet is firmly rooted in the same approximate time period as the ministry of Jesus in Roman-occupied Israel.

Stockbauer then provides some interesting biographical material on Hansen, recounting how, in 1918, Hansen was a college student spending her summer vacation with the Chippewa Indian tribe in Michigan.

"Her interest in their life was more than scholarly," Stockbauer writes. "Their language and dances, their culture and religion, struck a richly harmonic chord in her soul. Dark Thunder, the chief, shared much of the tribal knowledge and one day told her of a Holy Man who had visited the tribe in distant times. This man came to the Indians when their empire was united and great cities stretched for miles. Wherever he went, the miracles followed, and always he spoke of the Kingdom of His Father.

"In this brief story," Stockbauer continues, "Hansen sensed the germ of one much greater."

That summer, a council of many tribes gathered to tell the young student the holy legends. Her own gift to the council would be a book that preserved their words for future seekers after that holy truth. This marked the birth of "He Walked The Americas" – a book pursued over two continents during the course of 45 years – that would tell the story of a Miracle Worker, pale of feature, white-robed and with gray-green eyes that gazed into the future.

THE STAGE IN THE AMERICAS IS SET

According to Stockbauer, there is general agreement among scholars that the Americas were a thousand years ahead of their European counterparts at the dawn of the Christian era. In a way that is also characteristic of Hansen's groundbreaking work in the 1940s, Hansen cuts against the grain of popular misconceptions and declares America's indigenous peoples superior to the stereotypes that obscure their true nature behind a cloud of the white race's assumed "entitlement."

At the time, most of North America was united and spoke the common language Algonquin or Puan. The capital was at present-day Saint Louis and its most

THE SEARCH FOR THE "PALE PROPHET" IN ANCIENT AMERICA

sacred city was in Michigan. It was the civilization of the Mound Builders, whose artifacts and history were preserved in the Earth itself. Their streets and temples were lined with "the reach green carpets of strawberry vines. Their copper mines supplied three nations with a metal that was harder than steel," Stockbauer writes.

In Central America, the Toltec Empire flourished. Its capital was Tollan, which is believed to be present-day Teotihuacan, while its sacred city was Cholula. The Toltecs were master craftsmen who constructed magnificent temples and palaces and understood the sciences of the Earth and heavens. They were also exquisite artists who covered the walls of their buildings with splendidly colorful murals.

There was a similarly advanced culture in the high Andes of South America. Their gigantic and mysterious pictographs, so remarkable when seen from the air, are thought to originate from this time.

"As advanced as these cultures were," Stockbauer writes, "two practices threatened their stability – slavery and human sacrifice. These evils, with their attendant war and thievery, brought fear to the lives of the people. It was this great wound the Prophet had come to heal."

THE ITINERARY OF MERCY

The Prophet's journey began in Polynesia, where he appeared in the first glimmer of dawn. In this war-torn land, He admonished the people to forsake their weapons and resolve old hatreds. The people were ashamed that the first words spoken by this God were angry ones and they humbly bowed before Him. He spread His religion of love from island to island, and, when he left, the people were united. This unity of culture and tradition has persisted ever since.

From the islands He sailed east to Pachacamac in Peru. He found a jealous priesthood there who plotted His death. But He was protected wherever he went. He cleansed the temples and won the hearts of the people. There was much sadness when He left to teach the warring tribes of Brazil, but He gently said, "If you had a herd of llamas upon a hillside, and one little lamb fell into the canyon, would you not go down to still its crying? So I go to save my llamas, for that is my Father's business."

While Stockbauer for some reason doesn't point it out, this is a direct echo of Christ's words in Luke and Matthew, the Parable of the Lost Sheep. The version told in Luke 15, beginning with verse 3, reads: "What man of you, having a hundred sheep, if he has lost one of them, does not leave the ninety-nine in the wilderness and go after the one he has lost until he finds it? And when he has found it, he lays it on his shoulders, rejoicing. And when he comes home, he calls together his friends and neighbors, saying to them, 'Rejoice with me, for I have found my sheep which was lost.' Just so, I tell you, there will be more joy in heaven over one sinner who repents than over ninety-nine righteous persons who need no repentance."

THE SEARCH FOR THE "PALE PROPHET" IN ANCIENT AMERICA

The similarity between the fallen llama lamb example of the Prophet to the lost sheep parable of Jesus in the Gospel is not accidental but is instead one of the many fascinating correlations linking the two historical personages.

From Peru and Brazil, the Pale Prophet traveled north through the Caribbean and Gulf of Mexico, docking at seaports along the way. Here He received one of his many names – Hurukan, similar to our word "Hurricane" – when He calmed the winds of a deadly storm sweeping the land.

One may recall that Christ performs a similar miracle in the Gospel that also involved calming the wind and sea. The event is recorded in Matthew 8, beginning with verse 24, which reads: "And behold, there arose a great storm on the sea, so that the boat was being swamped by the waves; but he was asleep. And they went and woke him, saying, 'Save us, Lord; we are perishing.' And he said to them, 'Why are you afraid, O men of little faith?' Then he arose and rebuked the winds and the sea; and there was a great calm. And the men marveled, saying, 'What sort of man is this, that even winds and sea obey him?'"

Stockbauer writes that at this point in His history, many tribal leaders were afraid of His power, and as He traveled, his legend grew. Merchants would tell of his works, and traders would speak of the God who walked the Earth, healing the sick and taming the fiercest beast. Soon His name was whispered everywhere and many looked forward to his coming long before his sandaled feet had touched their land.

The Pale Prophet continued going north, up the Mississippi River to Canada. He is still remembered by the tribes He saw – the Cherokee, Chippewa, and Cree, the Algonquin, Dakota and Shawnee, the Pawnee, Choctaw and Seneca. Still they see His long white robe with black crosses at the hem. Fondly they recall how He always blessed the little children.

THE LOCAL LANGUAGES GIVE THE PROPHET MANY NAMES

Upon arrival, His first step was always to learn the local language, absorbing perhaps a thousand or more tongues of the indigenous peoples of the Americas. He refashioned the temples and renewed some of their ancient ceremonies. Child sacrifice became infant baptism. In the name of His Father, He taught the Golden Rule, sung in a cadence that resounded through the temples: "Do not kill or injure your neighbor, for it is not him that you injure; you injure yourself. Do good to him, thus adding to his days of happiness even as you then add to your own."

Wherever He stayed, He chose twelve disciples and carefully trained them in his new dispensation. His teachings would remain deeply interwoven in Native American life, a daily reminder of the lessons he imparted. He introduced people to seeds He had brought with Him and showed them new ways of planting while instructing them, "When the people are hungry, instead of making war, pray to

THE SEARCH FOR THE "PALE PROPHET" IN ANCIENT AMERICA

the Father that your needs be provided."

The Healer always silently prayed every morning before the dawn star appeared. This became His special star, and around its cycles He created a calendar for the people. The Book of Revelation, Chapter 22, verse 16, has Jesus declaring, "I am the root and the offspring of David, the bright morning star." So we have yet another correlation between first century Native American lore and the Bible. The consistencies between the two sources continue to increase.

As the Pale Prophet traveled, He always let the local people decide on their own name for Him. One tribe called Him "Wakea" or "Wakan," words for water meant to honor His mastery over water. To the Hopi, He was Tah-co-pah, which meant the Healer. The Seri tribe called Him Tlazoma – the Miracle Worker. The Cherokee named Him Ee-me-shee, the Wind God, and the Papago called Him E-see-cotl, — Great Healer. The Algonquin would not give Him their own name and asked instead for His childhood name when He lived across the ocean. So they called Him Chee-Zoos, meaning God of the Dawn Light.

In Central America, His most celebrated name was Quetzalcoatl, or the Plumed Serpent. The Quetzal was a rare and vivid green bird. "Co" stood for serpent, a symbol for water, and "tl" meant Lord. So He was known as the Lord of Wind and Water. The western Canadian tribes called Him after their highest mountain, Tacoma, to honor his name: Tla-acomah, Lord Miracle Worker.

The Seri of Baja, California, still tell of the time Tlazoma healed a blind man by placing wet sand in his eyes. Jesus uses a similar method in the Gospel of John, Chapter 9, beginning with verse one. Jesus encounters a man blind from birth. Jesus spits on the ground in order to make clay of the spittle then anoints the man's eyes with the clay. He instructs the man to wash his eyes clean in a nearby pool. "So he went and washed and came back seeing," the Gospel recounts. Again, the Seri story provides a marvelous consistency with the Biblical accounts.

When the Prophet came to Tollan, the capital of the Toltec Empire in central Mexico, His fame had come like a ghost before him.

THE OCEAN-LIKE ROAR OF ADULATION

According to Hansen's retelling of the ancient legend, "Already everywhere the people were waiting, covering the land up to the mountains, lining the highways, singing and chanting. The stories had brought out the masses from a thousand miles far-distant, and emptied all the towns and villages.

"Long had they known that He loved flowers, and now they filled the air with perfume, raining blossoms down upon Him. This rain grew thicker as He moved toward Tollan. Heavy flower carpets paved the highway. As soon as He walked over the blossoms, the people ran out and scrambled for them, hoping to keep a single petal which have borne His weight for a moment.

THE SEARCH FOR THE "PALE PROPHET" IN ANCIENT AMERICA

"At the gateway He paused a moment to gaze upon its fabulous beauty. Then He passed through the ponderous portals of metal, encrusted with their pearls and emerald, and from the throats of a million people came a roar like to an ocean, bursting through the mouths of the Toltecs as the monarch bowed low before Him and escorted Him into Tollan, the Golden.

"When He started to speak, a miracle happened. Never before to a great distance could the voice of one man be carried, but from the hilltop to beyond the city, to the wall and on to the mountains went forth His beautiful voice, His musical voice, speaking in Toltec."

This is all very similar to Jesus' triumphal entry into Jerusalem, the event now celebrated on Palm Sunday. When told by the Pharisees that he should rebuke his ecstatic followers, Jesus replied that even if their jubilant voices were made silent, "the very stones would cry out." The irrepressible joy of the moment could not be stilled by any human force.

Speaking that day to the Toltecs, He humbled every proud head. He would stay with the Toltecs many years, and it is thought that the Temple of the Sun at Teotihuacan and the Sacred Pyramid at Cholula were His special shrines where He instructed the priesthood in the ancient rites of initiation. His words and miracles had a profound effect on the thoughts and customs of the land, and, in peace and reconciliation, the Toltecs found their true power as a nation.

When He left Tollan, the Prophet journeyed east through the Yucatan and spent His last days in this hemisphere on the island of Cozumel. Then, in a magnificent redwood ship, He sailed into the sunrise, bound for His homeland across the sea.

TRUTH VERSUS MERE MYTH

"He departed," Stockbauer writes, "but the legend He left has taken many forms. Some have called it myth, but others are convinced of His historical identity."

There is, for example, Dr. Peter H. Buck, a Hawaiian scholar who thought the Prophet's clothing and the type of vessel He rode pointed to a Red Sea origin. Buck cited similar stories of a pale-skinned Teacher in the ancient stories of China, India and Japan. A mountain in Japan called Wakoyama is said to be named for the "white" god who taught there.

The Book of Mormon records events in America between 600 B.C. and 421 A.D. It has prophecies of Christ's coming and several chapters about His appearance in the Americas after His resurrection. As in the Bible and the Native American legends, He performs miracles and chooses twelve followers to continue His work.

Hansen herself thought the Teacher must have been a member of the

THE SEARCH FOR THE "PALE PROPHET" IN ANCIENT AMERICA

Essenes, a religious sect of early Christian times. Essenes wore a toga-like garment and always spoke of God as "My Father." Native Americans she interviewed knew the word Essene and their names for the Prophet – E-see-cotl and Ee-me-shee – may have been derivative of it.

THE SEARCH FOR THE "PALE PROPHET" IN ANCIENT AMERICA

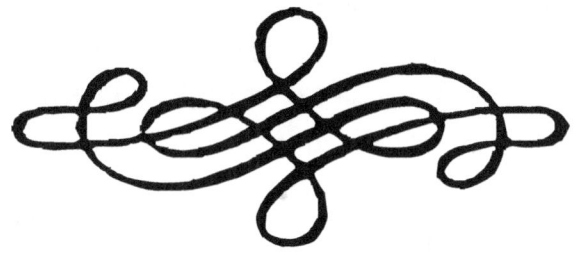

The Man/Woman Scholar Is Charged With A Mission

In the opening pages of "He Walked The Americas," Hansen quotes some of the Native Americans who first gave her the legends that would become the basis for the book.

"We are the ancients and our skin is red; with us, the Sacred Color," says Asa Delugie, War Chief of the Mescallero Apaches. "These are our legends told about the campfires on winter evenings. When you string them together, remember our great pride. Now we are looking down and our feathers are drooping. Tell the legends so that our young men will realize that the ancestor threads run in many directions. Through the tribes we have captured and with whom we have intermarried there is a red thread which runs back to the Red Land long sunken in the Destruction. Through some of our mothers there is a white thread to the words of The Prophet. Tell my young men to listen."

Asa Delugie is here charging Hansen with the mission of enlightening his future tribesmen regarding the Prophet's journey among their people. He also seems to be referring to lost Atlantis as the Red People's point of origin.

Meanwhile, Zeahley Tso, Chief of the Navajo, says, "This is our book. May you write it in beauty as we have told it in beauty." Again, Hansen has a duty to perform: doing justice to the beauty of the lore of the Prophet.

"There is evidence that some of our ancestors may have come from the ancient trading empire of Chan-Chan centuries before the rise of the Incan Power in Peru," says So-Sah-kuku, Chief Snake Priest of Oraibi. "Tell my people to learn of this great power which once ruled eyes. Tell them to look up and learn."

Perhaps the admonition to "look up and learn" has some connection to UFO sightings? Peru is home to the Nazca Lines, beautiful pictographs only visible from an airplane or helicopter.

THE SEARCH FOR THE "PALE PROPHET" IN ANCIENT AMERICA

"This is our book – these legends of ancient times," says Shooting Star of the Hunkapa Dacotah. "They are the blood which courses through our veins. We of the Seven Tribes of the Black Tortoise once had a Dream of Empire. Yet farther back through the cycles of time we knew the Great Wakon-Tah, but we forgot his words. These legends should help us to look up and remember."

The prideful claim to the true ownership of Hansen's book is repeated here, perhaps to compensate for the Native Americans' tragic loss of liberty and dignity. And was Shooting Star so named because of being witness to a UFO sighting? In any case, Hansen readily acknowledges that she is but a messenger for the Native Americans who seek to tell the world, both in her time and the unknowable future, that the Pale Prophet who walked among them was a racially colorblind vessel of mercy.

Polynesia: The Prophet's Journey Begins

The first stop on the journey of the Pale Prophet was an outlying island of the Tahitian group where two tribes were fighting bitterly.

THE FEARSOME ENTRANCE OF THE PALE ONE

"Once in the days long vanished," Hansen writes, "with three great ships which had sailed from the Sunset Lands [meaning the west, of course], came white-robed Wakea – the Fair God who healed the injured, raised the dead and walked on water."

The ships are further described as having giant sales like enormous birds with wings uplifted, glowing goldenly in the dawn light. As the ships moved closer to the island, where men were fighting for the possession of the good land, the warriors were suddenly frozen to immobility.

"What manner of monsters are these with the great wings?" they cried out. "Perhaps they have come to devour the people!"

The warriors forgot their battle. Friend and foe stood facing the sea, clutching their weapons in paralyzed fingers and staring in wide-eyed wonder. They saw something white moving toward them.

"Apparently it had come from the Great Birds," Hansen recounts, "and it glided easily over the water with the rhythmical ease of a man walking. As the spot of white came closer, they saw in amazement that this was a Fair God, man-like in form, but unlike their people. Soon they could see Him clearly, the gold of the dawn light shining behind and around Him, making a halo of His long, curling hair and beard. They saw the foam-like swish of His garments. As He came up on the wet sand, the warriors stared in fright at His garments; they were dry. Now they knew that a god stood among them, for none but gods can walk on water."

One of the most widely known of the miracles of Jesus was his walking on water. In the account given of the incident in Matthew 14, beginning with verse 22, Jesus had gone up to a mountain to pray in solitude and told the disciples to journey on by boat ahead of him. "When evening came, he was there alone, but the boat by this time was many furlongs distant from the land, beaten by the waves; for the wind was against them. And in the fourth watch of the night, he came to them, walking on the sea. But when the disciples saw him, they were terrified, saying, 'It is a ghost!' And they cried out for fear. But immediately he spoke to them, saying, 'Take heart, it is I; have no fear.'"

The points in common between the Polynesian legend and the Gospel are particularly obvious here. Not only do the Pale Prophet and Jesus both walk on the water, in each case the miracle also terrifies those who see it. Just as the island warriors are paralyzed with fear, so are the disciples frightened to the extent that Jesus must reassure them that he is not a ghost or some kind of malevolent apparition.

PRAYING FOR THE STRANGER'S FORGIVENESS

The island warriors became transfixed by the mysterious stranger's grey-green eyes, which flashed with anger.

"A god had come from the sea to walk among them," Hansen writes, "and His first look was that of anger! The warriors fell down as one man and began an old chant anciently employed to a god for forgiveness. When they dared again to raise up their own eyes, they saw Him going among the injured and dying who rose from their pain to find themselves well of body as soon as His hand or His garments had touched them."

Everyone is aware of Christ's power to heal the sick and dying, but there is a scriptural precedent for his garment seeming to have a healing power of its own. In Matthew, Chapter 9, beginning with verse 20, "And behold, a woman who had suffered from a hemorrhage for twelve years came up behind him and touched the fringe of his garment; for she said to herself, 'If I only touch his garment, I shall be made well.' Jesus turned, and seeing her he said, 'Take heart, daughter; your faith has made you well.' And instantly the woman was made well."

On the Polynesian island, villagers began arriving with presents for the Pale Prophet, creeping on their knees out of fear of His powers. Small boats began to disembark from the Great Birds, bringing other strangers similar in appearance to the Prophet, also with beards but dressed in colored clothes unlike the white mantle of their leader, for whom they felt an obvious reverence and love.

"Friend and foe among the Polynesians now set about to entertain the strangers," Hansen writes. "Putting forth their choicest dishes, making welcome with songs and dances, they invited the strangers to partake of the great feast."

As the sun begins to set, the strangers appear to be preparing to leave, which causes the islanders great sadness. But their joy returns when they realize the Pale Prophet himself was planning no journey but would remain among them after His fellow travelers had said their tearful goodbyes.

"Then, after many further embraces," Hansen writes, "they watched the strangers enter the small boats and row back to the great Bird-Ships. The great ships were nevermore seen by the tribesmen."

THE LAW OF LOVE

Wakea, as the Polynesians named the Prophet, learned the island language so quickly it amazed the natives. He began to teach the people about the One God who ruled the heavens, who spoke through the volcanoes and who breathed on the ocean. It seems very likely that Wakea/Jesus would begin their instruction by introducing the Biblical, monotheistic view of God. He also taught them that war was not of God's making, for His law was Love One Another.

"For Wakea, they gave up war and the sacrifice of children," Hansen writes. "Then the men carried Him with them, taking Wakea from island to island so each could meet the strange Fair God whose hands were miracles of healing. Many then were the songs of Wakea and many the legends, which down the long vistas of time have been forgotten. Yet his name has never been forgotten."

THE SAD GOODBYE

After some days, the Prophet began to look toward the east and ask questions about the Lands of the Dawn Star. The people were loath to lose the Healer, and, as long as they could, they tried to dissuade His growing wish to travel eastward. Yet they loved him too much to deny His desire, so they began preparations for the long journey. Wakea promised to return like he had come, through the light of the dawning, if the people kept his commandments and always loved one another.

"Thus from the islands and into the sunrise rode the long boats carrying Wakea," Hansen writes, "beautiful creature of peace and laughter whose curling brown hair trapped the red-gold of sunlight and whose strange level eyes held the sea's deepest mystery. So the Fair God moved into dawn, sped onward by the chants of farewell sung by the sorrowing people. And since that day, though some have said that He is sometimes seen in spirit, yet in the flesh they are still waiting for Him to come back to his beloved islands of Polynesia."

This Polynesian belief in a physical Second Coming of the Fair God is wholly consistent with the Gospel accounts. When Christ appears to the disciples after his resurrection, he presents himself in a material form that the doubting Apostle Thomas can touch, as in the well-known story of Thomas touching the crucifixion wounds in the Savior's hands. Also, the New Testament prophecies of Christ's Second Coming clearly refer to his physical return from the skies leading an army of angels and saints to do battle with the antichrist and his assembled armies. Again, the physical nature of the event is a given.

THE SEARCH FOR THE "PALE PROPHET" IN ANCIENT AMERICA

CORRESPONDENCE WITH A RENOWNED ANTHROPOLOGIST

At the end of the chapter on Polynesia, Hansen tells of consulting Dr. Peter H. Buck, the half-Maori author of "Vikings of the Sunrise" and a world-renowned authority on the history of the Polynesian peoples. She asked Buck if he knew of a prophet or teacher wearing a white toga-like garment who had come to the islands teaching theology and agriculture.

"I recognize this figure from our legends," Buck replied in a letter to Hansen. "His name is Wakea. Wakea, the Healer, lived in the first century of the Christian era, or, generally speaking, in the time of Jesus. It seems that He came in the early dawning of our history to these tribes who were fighting in this outlying island. I am enclosing a copy of the story as it was told to me."

So the legends and lore are gathered and passed from native to scholar and on to other scholars. The story of the Pale Prophet next moves on to Peru, another locale where memories of Him still linger after two thousand years.

Peru, Brazil and Guatemala: The Mission of Mercy Continues

The Pale One's mission of mercy took him to Peru and a city of ancient glory called Pachacmac, queen of the ocean. There, on a glittering temple dedicated to the Fish God, stood He who was called Wakea by some and by others Wako.

"His temple," Hansen writes, "built by the wealth of the ages, dated back so far into forgotten time that men no longer remembered its building. Now the long rays of the morning sunlight caught it up in dazzling splendor, lit its tiers of jet, high-polished, alternating with crested gold work, and rising above the quiet city like a glorious pyramid-mountain. Upon the summit stood the Pale One, beard and hair and robe gold-tinted, as was the incense which swirled above Him with its scent of burning cedar."

Here Hansen demonstrates an ability to write descriptive passages like a practiced writer of fiction, a technique that was years ahead of its time. It would not be until the 1960s, when writers like Tom Wolfe and Norman Mailer began to combine straight reporting with narratives and descriptive writing more normally employed by a novelist, that what was then called the "New Journalism" came into fashion.

THE TEMPLE IS CLEANSED

As the Pale One stood atop the temple, the people danced in ceremony beneath Him. At last He spoke in a voice "deeply resonant like a golden stream flowing."

"As I watched you, oh my people," He began, "I thought again of how I landed upon your shores and came to the temple. The priesthood, crafty and deceitful, would have slain me for their idols, but they could not, and their knives fell from their fingers. I ordered the temple to be cleared of idols, and behold! The restless ocean arose, and with foaming fingers cleansed the temple and left it shining."

When Jesus Christ's ministry brought him to the temple in Jerusalem, he also faced a priesthood that was "crafty and deceitful" – the Pharisees, the religious authority of the Jews. In Matthew 21, verse 12, we read: "And Jesus entered the temple of God and drove out all who sold and bought in the temple, and he overturned the tables of the money-changers and the seats of those who sold pigeons. He said to them, 'It is written, "My house shall be called a house of prayer," but you make it a den of robbers.'"

The fact that the Healer speaks of the cleansing of the temple in Peru is neatly echoed by the story in the Gospel, though the method employed – the risen ocean in one version and the simple physical act of an indignant Jesus in the other – is different.

The Pale One continued speaking to the gathered multitude about the changes He had wrought for them.

"I found you sinful in cunning warfare," He said, "and I leave you peaceful and contented. I found you dealing in human slavery; I leave you free. My well-trained priesthood will carry on all rites for me. Baptismal, marriage and the last interment – all will go on. Why am I going? Because there are wild tribes in the jungles. They know not of the One Great Spirit who rules all men. They follow him not. They still wage warfare."

LODGES IN THE FATHER'S LAND

And so He journeyed to Brazil, where Hansen describes Him sitting in the Council House of the Chieftain nestled in a jungle that is a wonderland of green flora. Again, He summarizes the progress He has made with the people there.

"For twelve moons I have walked among you while the sun swung around his circle," the Fair Prophet said. "For ten moons now you have not battled or taken human sacrifices. I brought you seeds and you have used them; seeds for drugs and food and clothing, spices and the warm sweet chocolate, as well as gourds for good containers. I taught you many ceremonies, baptismal rites and sacred marriage. I leave behind those who can lead you, for I must go on to other nations."

The chieftain then stands and speaks of the day of the Healer's departure as one of darkness for the natives. The Pale One then assures him that, "In my Father's Land you will all have lodges, and beyond the veil I await your coming."

Jesus says something nearly identical in the Gospel of John, chapter 14, verse 1: "Let not your hearts be troubled; believe in God, believe also in me. In my Father's house are many rooms; if it were not so, would I have told you that I go to prepare a place for you? And when I go and prepare a place for you, I will come again and will take you to myself, that where I am you may be also."

The Pale One then tells His listeners in Brazil, "Return not to your ways of evil; I ask but this: your faithful promise."

The chieftain responds by saying, "Hear this, O Blessed Master. So that our sons will never forget thee, and forever keep thy teachings, we shall renounce the names we have carried, and to the eternity beyond tomorrow shall be known as the Waikanoes: Faithful followers of the Master."

Hansen concludes the Brazilian chapter by simply noting that "The Waikanoes are a non-Christian wild tribe from Matto Grosso." The name may have persisted, but the obedience to Christian precepts apparently did not.

A TERRIFYING HEALING

The Prophet traveled on to Guatemala in Central America.

"Among the tall smoking volcanoes," Hansen writes, "among the mountains went the Healer, seeking out the ever-warring tribes, takers of men, the Sacrificers. He brought them seeds and lectured to them, speaking of the One Great Spirit."

It is while visiting a village in Guatemala that the Prophet performed a healing.

"A little child came running to Him, crying," Hansen recounts. "Its clothes were torn and its body bleeding, clawed by the sharp claws of the jaguar. He picked the child up, and, turning to the stream bed, knelt and washed away the blood stains. The people following in consternation saw no more the marks of the jaguar. The child was well and clean and smiling. But when He held the baby to them, the people backed away in terror."

The frightened natives said the baby was accursed and that the healing was a sign that their idol Balaam was angry.

There is a similar moment told of in Matthew, Chapter 9, beginning with verse 32: "As they were going away, behold, a dumb demoniac was brought to him. And when the demon had been cast out, the dumb man spoke; and the crowds marveled, saying, 'Never was anything like this seen in Israel.' But the Pharisees said, 'He casts out demons by the prince of demons.'"

In both instances, a holy miracle is called an unholy one and attributed to an evil power.

The Healer tells the Guatemalan natives that the child is not accursed but is blessed instead. He also chides them for fearing Balaam.

"Think you the anger of this creature is greater than My Father's goodness?" He asks the throng. "Your Balaam is not so powerful; he must be fed the blood of children! My Father needs no man to feed him, yet He gives plants to feed a mortal."

But the very man the Healer was rebuking pointed a trembling finger. The Healer turned to face the jaguar, its lemon eyes upon Him. The Pale One placed the child on the ground behind Him and stepped toward the great cat as He held His arm up in a sign of peace.

He spoke to the jaguar, saying, "Soft-footed Chief, in thy jungle setting, come close to receive My Father's blessing. Forgiven though art for the pangs of thy hunger. Go and claw no more little children."

When the Pale One tells the jaguar, "Go and claw no more little children," one is reminded of the famous incident in which Christ admonishes an angry mob bent on stoning a woman guilty of adultery. Christ tells the gathering of would-be executioners, "Let him who is without sin among you be the first to throw a stone at her." The mob departs, and Jesus is left alone with their intended victim. He says to her, "Go, and do not sin again." The story is found in John, Chapter 8, beginning with verse one.

After the Healer addresses the jaguar in kindness and amazes the natives with His bravery, the fierce animal lay down before the Pale One "and rolled, catlike, to show its pleasure, inviting the caress of those slim, pale fingers. The people, watching, fell down to worship. To this day, among the wild tribes within the canyons and the mountains of the land called Guatemala, the story is oft-repeated."

ATTEMPTED MURDER BY THE HIGH PRIEST

The Prophet went on to Ek-Balaam, a Guatemalan city whose precise location is no longer remembered. Here the priesthood of the Tiger waited to deceive and kill Him. Like the Pharisees who tested Jesus, the priests of Ek-Balaam set out to trap the Pale One.

"We will offer to Him a captive," they said. "If He takes the sacrifice, He is silenced, for He goes against all His teachings. Yet, if He does not, we will declare Him but man and kill Him, and break His body over the idol."

As the Healer journeyed on to Ek-Balaam, He was greeted joyfully by all who saw Him. They covered His path with flowers and cried His name as they brought to Him their sick and injured. He entered the mighty city with the multitudes forming a torrent behind Him.

"He thrust aside the jeweled gateway with a gesture of derision," Hansen writes. "The first of the mob now seemed reluctant, for this was the courtyard of the Bloody Tiger. Yet the Prophet had neither stopped nor looked behind Him, so the people burst in and swirled around Him. Quietly, He ascended the dreaded stairway. Halfway up, He was met by the blood-smeared black-robed high priest of the Tiger."

The cunning priest challenged the Prophet, saying, "No man dares climb these steps of the Blood God! Come you as a man or a god from the Great Veil?"

The Prophet answered, saying, "I come to you in the name of My Father – the one and only god of mankind. I bid you cease these sacrifices."

"Then you come as a god," the priest replied, "and we welcome you as one. We bring unto you now a sacrifice to show you that we know you."

As the priests stood waiting, the people gasped in mortal terror at the daring of the Prophet. This was the signal for the priests to drag a chained captive forward, whom they forced to kneel before the Pale One. Before the priest could raise the blade of sacrifice, the Prophet touched the victim and his chains were shattered.

"Arise, my friend, and join the people," the Prophet said.

The people stared in wonderment, but not the High Priest, who brandished his blade and started toward the Prophet screaming: "Thou art not god! You are a demon who fooled us. You cannot feed on life-blood! You are but a man with human pity! Die as men die – for the Tiger!"

The Pale One raised His palms and the High Priest saw in each one a large cross torn in the flesh. The High Priest stood as one transfixed.

"Why not strike down with the knife and kill me?" the Prophet asked his would-be murderer. "Ye cannot? Why do ye tremble?"

Then He turned and spoke to the people, saying that he brought a message from "the God who has no image. He dwells beyond the rainbow. He lives in the lava, moves in the oceans, breathes in the windstorm and made all things from ant to tiger."

He told the people they had to make a choice.

"There are but two trails to follow," he said. "One is the Way of My Father and one is the Way of the Jungle. You have chosen to follow the latter. Think you there is power in that image? That rock has only the power that you give it."

To make His point, the Prophet picked up the fallen sacrificial knife and smashed it upon the face of the idol.

"That is how strong your Law of the Jungle is," He continued, "the eat or be eaten, kill or be tortured – death ends all and so let us forget it and obey the law of our stomachs! You think of yourselves as strong men who crush and take from a weaker neighbor. Stop and look down the vistas of history. Where are the nations who lived by the Jungle? Where is the world-encircling power of the Serpents? It was crushed by the flood of My Father's making. Where are your strong men who lived by evil? They face judgment for breaking the Great Law of My Father, greater than all earthly precepts.

"That law is this: Love One Another."

THE SEARCH FOR THE "PALE PROPHET" IN ANCIENT AMERICA

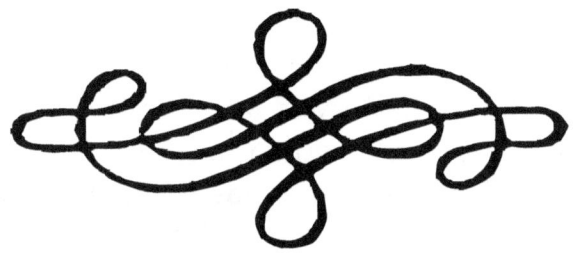

The Heartless Queen of the Yucatan

After His visit to Ek-Balaam, where the priest had attempted to murder Him, the Healer went to the Yucatan, also called "The Land of the Woman" because it was ruled by a queen who was lovely, with her skin the color of old ivory and hair as blue as the wing of a raven. Her hands were as smooth as the skin of a baby, yet she ruled with a fist of iron with none able to oppose her in her cruelty and heartlessness.

THE EVIL ONES MAKE THEIR PLANS

By this time, the Pale One was famous throughout the Americas; the queen and her cohorts began to anticipate His arrival.

"If we do not greet this stranger," the queen told her courtiers, "the people may turn at last against us, for they think Him divine. As you know, they have named Him, among other titles, the Lord of Wind and Water. On the other hand, if we do entertain Him, and allow Him to fashion a temple, He may change our manner of living or so devoutly win the people that they will no longer obey us. Therefore we cannot entertain Him."

The courtiers began to shout for the Prophet's death, but there was no working method for killing Him. If they simply attacked Him violently, He was known to freeze His would-be assailants in a trance. If they fired arrows at Him, He could command the wind and air to obey Him. If they used the weapon of the Serpent, a poisoned lance, He could walk on water.

"You mean there is no way to kill Him?" the courtiers asked, abashed.

The queen said there was a way that they had not considered: to invite the Healer to dinner at the palace, giving Him the seat of honor at the table.

"When He arises to speak to us," the queen continued, "the guard at the door knows my signal. As usual, it is to be the clap of my two hands. That will signify the trapdoor is to be released. He will find Himself in a dungeon, and from this one, as you well know, no man in all of our history has ever come forth into the land of the living."

THE ANGRY FIRE GOD

After the plans of the wicked were laid, the Prophet entered the city with the adoring people raining down flowers upon Him. The queens' army greeted Him and escorted Him to the palace. He was given a luxurious room and clean clothes to wear. That afternoon, as He stood on the palace rooftop to address the people, the mountain over the city began to belch dark smoke from its summit.

The people were afraid, murmuring among themselves, "Why is the Fire God angry? Is it because He comes among us?"

But the Pale One raised His arm in His sign of Peaceful Greeting and blessed the mountain. He told the people of its beauty, with its hair of ice and its soft cloud blankets. He told them to make their lives beautiful so that when they came to the Land of Shadows there would be no unhappy things to remember.

GLOATING LAUGHTER BECOMES HORRIFIED SCREAMING

"That night," Hansen writes, "all went as planned at the banquet. The Healer was given the seat of honor. No one seemed to notice that He spoke very little, that He toyed with His food but did not eat it. And when at last the eating was finished, with all the laughter and entertainment, the Prophet arose and stared at the courtiers. From face to face went the gray-green eyes, until the silence lingered into unnaturalness. Then suddenly the woman arose. Staring imperiously upon Him, she clapped her ivory smooth hands and the Prophet fell into the dungeon."

The woman began to laugh gloatingly and was soon joined by her guards and courtiers.

"Yea, thus had spoken the woman – then spoke the mountain," Hansen writes. "With a crash heard into the enemy kingdoms, the whole top of the mountain exploded! Gone was its headdress of ice-white feathers! Gone were the soft cloud blankets! And as the tiger shakes the monkey, so the mountains shook the city!"

Within the palace, which only moments before had rung with laughter, the courtiers screamed in fear and clung to one another in an insane desperation. Only the queen and a single guard escaped. The queen ran screaming down the corridors, still hearing the horrified shrieks of the dying. The people tumbled into the streets and saw the Prophet gazing quietly at the mountain. A guard from the palace, injured and burned in those moments of terror, crawled abjectly toward the Healer, babbling incoherently and pointing to the ruins of the palace.

"Into the streets staggered the people," Hansen writes, "carrying their injured and crying children, gazing in unbelief at the mountain, a flaming torch against the heavens, lighting the city like a red sun or a monstrous fiery fountain, flinging upward stars of fury which danced grotesquely about the crimson moon and returned to earth in a blazing curtain."

BUILDING A PYRAMID-TEMPLE TO HONOR THE DESTRUCTION

But the Pale One stood on the ruins of the palace, His robe untouched by the rain of cinders. He waved the people toward Him and began to lead them away from the city as they stumbled in the thickening fog of ashes. The Prophet and the people walked all night long, stopping only for Him to heal their wounds and stroke the burned ones, making whole the flesh beneath His fingers. Then on they journeyed to the land of Panuco, near a mighty river, where they stopped and built another city. Here a great pyramid-temple was dedicated to the Prophet and the mountain.

"To this day," writes Hansen, "in the land of Panuco, one can still hear the legend of how the Healer came to the Land of the Woman and was saved from death by the flaming mountain. The Place of Destruction is called the Land of the Red Moon, and the ruins are untouched by the spades of strangers."

THE QUEEN REMAINS BEHIND AS A TORMENTED GHOST

If one wins the trust of the local natives, they will tell a curious story: When the moon is full, strange things happen at the Place of Destruction. Strangers who go there and stay through the night, when the moon lights up the desolation, swear they can look into the Palace. There, a torch is crazily swinging as if still heaving from an earthquake, and a woman is heard madly running followed by wild peals of laughter that echo throughout the ruined city and then give way to shrieks of horror. No stranger will stay there more than one night, and witnesses to the haunting always hurriedly leave the country.

Hansen then complains that she was unable to confirm the story because none of the indigenous people could be induced by gifts or money to lead her to the Place of Destruction when the moon is full and the Woman is laughing. She believes it may be possible that the original location has been forgotten down through the many ages.

She also notes that there are two versions of this legend. In one, the Woman was banished to the Land of the Red Moon, where she became insane. That version, Hansen feels, is more "garbled" and less complete in its story. Therefore this version, which explains the name "Land of the Red Moon," seems more logical and was the one chosen to be included in "He Walked The Americas."

THE SEARCH FOR THE "PALE PROPHET" IN ANCIENT AMERICA

The Future, a Lost Fawn and the Prophet's Birth

It was when he had traveled to what is now called Etowa, Georgia, that the Prophet first mentioned the future. He stood high above the people, staring off into the horizon as He spoke.

"Afar off through time," He said, "my spirit is walking down the cycles of the future. I see the armies of the Serpents moving northward from their cities, being driven out by bloody warfare. These ancient worshippers of the Fire have returned to the ways of their fathers and once more are sacrificing to idols. They are coming up the river, the Serpents led by the Turtle."

Civil war and anarchy would result. If the warring peoples could convert once again to the Peace religion of the One God, the outcome might be different. But the Prophet knew such a reprieve would not likely happen. Senseless warfare was the inevitable result.

"Farther off, there is another invasion," He continued. "In ships, many bearded men are coming from across the Sunrise [Atlantic] Ocean. Many are the ships as the snowflakes of winter. I see these men taking the Broad Land; and the Mounds which hold the crests of our cities are for them – alas! – but earth for the taking. They do not respect our trees of cedar. They are but hungry, unenlightened children, and with them the vision closes."

The Prophet is clearly seeing a vision of the invading Spanish, whose ships would not arrive for a millennium and a half to carry out their genocide and pillaging of the indigenous peoples.

Hansen writes, "Many southern tribes, now in Oklahoma, still remember this prediction first spoken at the temple in Georgia so long ago in times long vanished. Choctaw, Cherokee, Chickasaw and Creek – do your children still remember? Or have the old chants been forgotten as they have among so many others?"

THE SEARCH FOR THE "PALE PROPHET" IN ANCIENT AMERICA

A "CHARMING" HEALING

The following incident was said to have taken place in what is now West Virginia.

"One of the most charming of all the Prophet legends," Hansen writes, "is that told by the Cherokee Nation. Once, as the Healer walked in the forest, deeply troubled by thoughts of the future, He came upon a fawn in a pool of moonlight. Its coat was blue and silver, its legs were weak, for it was hungry and could not find its mother."

The Healer spoke to it: "Silver-flecked babe of the forest, where is thy mother? Which path did she take when she left thee?"

The fawn looked at him sorrowfully then turned toward a dark path. Without hesitation, the Prophet followed. Soon they came to a bower where the mother lay among the leaves, having been clawed unmercifully by a huge forest cat. She had led the fierce animal away from her child, offering herself as a victim to save her fawn.

The Healer knelt beside the mother and gently stroked her torn and bleeding body until at last she stood erect beside Him. His disciples, who had been following at a distance to ensure his safety, saw the miracle happen and stared in disbelief as the doe nuzzled her fawn. The disciples asked the Prophet whether healing an animal might not waste power better used on a human being.

"Nay," smiled the Pale One. "There cannot be too many good deeds. Such is the manner of compassion. A lost lamb is My Father's business, as important as saving a nation, if one need not choose between them. More precious in My Father's eyes is a good deed than the most exquisite jewel."

His disciples knelt to touch His white robe, where the dark crosses stood out in the moonlight.

THE PROPHET TELLS OF HIS BIRTH

When He had come to Oklahoma, which translates as the Land of the Red Man, He was asked by His priesthood to speak to them of His childhood.

"He told them that He was born across the ocean," Hansen writes, "in a land where all men were bearded. In this land He was born of a virgin on a night when a bright star came out of the heavens and stood over His city. Here, too, the heavens opened and down came winged beings singing chants of exquisite beauty."

Hansen next reports on excavations made in Oklahoma by a team of archeologists.

"When the University of Oklahoma was digging in the Spiro Mound," she writes, "much pottery was discovered which showed winged beings singing. Here also was the hand with the cross through the palm, about which the professors were deeply puzzled. They still have no explanation as they stare at these things

THE SEARCH FOR THE "PALE PROPHET" IN ANCIENT AMERICA

in their museums."

It is extremely uncanny that the university archeologists should discover pottery artifacts that seem to confirm the legends of the singing creatures with wings that came down from above to honor the Pale One as He spoke of His birth to the Native Americans.

Meanwhile, around the campfires of the ancients, the tales of the Prophet are secret. For the benefit of their youth, they chant the stories of long ages ago when they lived in the cities and of a sainted Healer who came and lived among them.

"To them, He was known as Chee-Zoos, the Dawn God," Hansen writes, "and they whisper of Him about the campfires on winter evenings when no white man can listen. The love they bear Him is beyond measurement, for well they know He watches over them. And when their journey is over, He will meet them in the Land of Shadows, for such was His sacred promise. They smoke the sacred peace pipe in His memory and blow the smoke to the four directions, knowing that to each man comes his retribution, no matter how flows the river of history."

Hansen explains that trusting in the Prophet's promises gives the Red Man great pride in spite of the dire poverty that nowadays stalks him and the starvation that sits at his table.

"In the masklike calm of his expression," Hansen writes, "there smiles a secret satisfaction, something that to puzzled white men is entirely beyond understanding."

Hansen advises the reader to further explore the many scientific reports on the Spiro Mound in Oklahoma. A wealth of relevant data has been unearthed there and one can learn a great deal about the spiritual beliefs of the ancients who first possessed the land.

Another point to ponder is the idea that some of the indigenous people in Hansen's time kept their knowledge of the Pale One secret from the White Man. Even though their faith in the reality of the Prophet and the salvation He had promised them was unshakable, it would somehow spoil things if the White Man understood their devotion to, ironically, essentially the same entity the White Man felt had blessed him as he conquered the peoples of the Americas.

Whose faith was more real, more sincerely bound up in adoration for the miraculous and the divine? One hesitates only a moment before answering that the Red Man's faith in the Pale One seems to exceed the White Man's faith in Jesus simply because the Red Man is both more needful and more deserving.

The Angry Prophet Among the Pawnee

"The Pawnee remember the Prophet," writes Hansen, "who came and taught them of His Father: the Mighty Holy One of the Heavens. He told them not to forsake His precepts, and, when they returned again to warfare, they thought often of His predictions, of how war but breeds more carnage. Even then He foretold the coming of the white man. The Pawnee remember Him as Paruxti and His Father as Tirawa. They know that they disobeyed Him and they pray to Him in anguish.

"Many tribes have tales of the Healer," she continues, "and how at one time He came among them. Few did He miss, no matter how distant or poor or lost in the ways of other religions. But to the Pawnee He came twice – the last time in anger."

Some wild young braves of the Puanee (the tribe today known as the Pawnee) formed a secret league to prey on the country, planning to make themselves rich by attacking area merchants traveling up and down the Mississippi River. The rebellious young men had also returned to the old war-religion and gave the merchants they captured to the Fire God in exchange for their idol's protection.

One night the aggregate of thieves and idolaters lay in wait for the longships of the merchants, who were stopping their journey for the night, intending to sleep in the forest. They suspected no mischief and posted no watch since the Pawnee were long known to be a peaceful tribe. The group of merchants made camp and conversed, remembering the long trip and the girls in distant cities. They also spoke of the man in the flowing white mantle and the awe inspiring miracles He had accomplished. But one youth among them was a skeptic.

"It is strange that we always seem to miss Him," the young man sighed, "for I would like to see Him – this creature that we call the Dawn God, and others the

Lord of Wind and Water."

The talk around the campfire became hushed, and the group passed the sacred tobacco pipe to one another. At last each got out his blankets and was soon asleep.

Then, yelling like Skiri the Grey Wolf, the wild Pawnee leaped upon the sleeping merchants. The surprised prisoners were forced to carry their own trade goods back to the camp of the bandits. The Pawnee were in a frenzy of madness, leaping and yelling as they staked out two men for the fire-death, for sacrifices to the Fire God. Savage was the untamed dancing as they lit the flames around their captives.

"Only one old man protested," Hansen writes. "He pointed to the East where the Star of the Morning was rising, but the young men paid no attention. Who cared about the Star of the Morning? No one but the One they had called the Healer when first He had come to see them. But now that One was far away and His magic was weak here. So they went on chanting the wolf-song. Laughingly, they pointed at the prisoners. One was dead and another dying."

The young men taunted the old man, saying, "Let Him come and revive these men! That would be much better magic than stopping a windstorm or walking on water!"

Then the eastern sky lit up with fire and everyone turned in wonder as the consternation silenced the chanting. Suddenly, He appeared among them! Like a creature from another planet, shining with a strange resonance, each hair of His head luminescent, a weird glow rippling from his garments and His eyes flashing with lightning, He stood staring at the Pawnee People.

"Is this the way you keep my commandments? Is this the manner of your insult to the Spirit called Tir-aw-wa? I come to shield you from His anger, or lo, a great wind would ignite the forest! And to ashes would be consigned the Pawnee Nation!"

While the Pawnee stared at Him, the young men frozen in fear, a weak voice cried out from the fire, saying, "Chee-Zoos, Master! From these flames, release me!"

The Healer turned and looked at the tortured man and said, "You are free, my son. Walk away from the fire."

The burned man moved and the chains dropped from around him. Then he staggered toward the Healer, falling and clutching the hem of the white robe embroidered with its line of crosses. Those who watched were witnessing a miracle, one which they had said could not happen, as the burned man rose up without a blemish.

Nor was the scene finished, for the Prophet next walked toward the dead man, saying, "Arise! Another day is dawning. Thou art not yet for the Land of Shadows! Arise and return to the Land of the Living."

The fire died away, and the blackened corpse stirred and lifted its head and its burned arms.

"Arise, my son. No chains are on thee," the Pale One said. "Come toward me and be made whole in body, for such this day is the will of My Father!"

The man arose and walked out of the ashes, staring at his restored flesh with incredulous eyes as he repeatedly murmured, "To think that I had questioned thy power – forgive, my Master, an unbeliever."

There is a similar moment in the Gospel of Mark, chapter 9, beginning with verse 20, in which a demon-possessed young boy is brought by his father to Jesus in the hope that the Messiah can cast the devil out.

"And Jesus asked his father, 'How long has he had this?' And he said, 'From childhood. And it has often cast him into the fire and into the water, to destroy him; but if you can do anything, have pity on us and help us.' And Jesus said to him, 'If you can! All things are possible to him who believes.' Immediately the father of the child cried out and said, 'I believe; help my unbelief!'"

Mark records that Jesus then rebuked the unclean spirit. After crying out and convulsing the boy one last time, the demon left the boy as commanded.

The idea of belief and faithlessness existing simultaneously in the human mind is expressed both by the stricken father in the Gospel of Mark and the native merchant in Hansen's story who awakens to find himself risen from the dead and healed of his burns. Even the words with which they each give voice to this confused state of mind is nearly identical.

After the Pale One had carried out His Father's will, the Pawnee gazed on the scene in silence, feeling the shame and terror of a child lost and bewildered, according to Hansen.

"Yet down through the ages has come the story," she writes, "and sometimes the old ones repeat it on winter evenings beside the camp fire: the legend of the Son of Mighty Tirawa, who came back in anger on a shaft of the dawn light, and, by His presence, saved from extinction the entire Pawnee Nation."

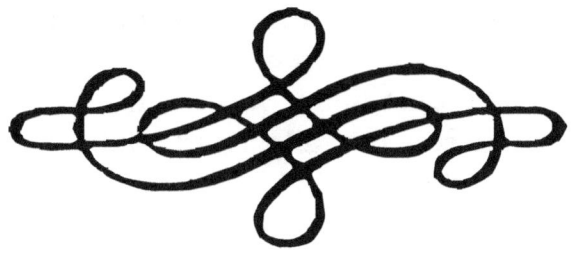

Teaching the Ways of Peace

When the Prophet heard tales of the Sunrise Ocean, what we call the Atlantic, and the Five Tribes of Warring nations, he expressed an immediate desire to see them, for the Healer was much opposed to war. So He traveled with the merchants across the mighty Alleghenies, coming to the Seneca Nation where He called the chieftains into council.

The Pale God spoke to them at length on the ways of His Father, as he had throughout His travels in the Americas. As always, He spoke the peoples' language with great ease as He explained His Peace Religion. Then He asked them bluntly: What was the reason for their warfare?

"The Fire Chieftains were embarrassed," the legend goes, "for they had long forgotten the reason, if indeed they ever had a reason. Each warrior looked upon the other and none could think of a valid answer. Therefore He bound them ceremonially into a never-ending alliance. To each He gave a sacred duty to perform for the alliance, and then He asked them to smoke the Peace Pipe, filled with tobacco and cedar shavings, and to blow the smoke to the four directions, making the sign of the Great Cross, which is a holy symbol.

"Never from that time onward," the legend continues, "have the Five Nations fought each other, nor has the trust He gave them been cracked and broken."

There are many moments in the Gospels when Christ talks of peace. Matthew Chapter 5, verse 9, reads "Blessed are the peacemakers, for they shall be called sons of God." In Luke, Chapter 1, verse 79, Zechariah prophesies of the as-yet-unborn John the Baptist that he was coming to prepare the way for Jesus in order for the savior "to give light to those who sit in darkness and in the shadow of death, to guide our feet into the way of peace." In John, Chapter 14, verse 27, Jesus tells his disciples, "Peace I leave with you; my peace I give to you; not as the world gives do I give to you. Let not your hearts be troubled, neither let them be afraid."

At the council in Seneca, one chieftain was particularly tall and had a lofty stature, so that he "could easily look down on the heads of the others. Indeed, the Prophet was not a short man, but neither was He as tall as the chieftain. The Seneca chieftain, seeing that he was the tallest and could look over the light hair of the Pale God, rose and waited to speak."

In a kind of shocked silence, the others waited to see if he would presume to question the Prophet.

The tall chieftain looked at the Healer and said, "I have been watching you while you were speaking, oh One whom the people call the Dawn God. It is true that you hold a most strange fascination over the minds of men. I know that the people call you the Dawn God. If it is true, then you can prove it. Meet me here in four days in the early morning before the sun has shot his first long red arrow, and we shall stand before this door together. If the first red arrow of the dawn light touches your hair before it paints my eagle feather, then indeed you are the Dawn God. This I give to you as a challenge. Now, for this day, I have spoken."

The others looked at the Prophet, who sat still, as if in deep thought, then finally rose to speak.

The Pale One accepted the challenge and agreed to meet the chieftain at the place and time the Senecan had designated. During the four days, the Healer went among the people, not speaking of His appointment, though everyone knew he would keep it, for the Great One never broke a promise.

At the time appointed, large crowds swarmed around the Great Lodge, where the contest was to be held. First to climb the mound was the Prophet, who spoke to the assembled nations as the first golden shafts of the Dawn Star became visible. It is said that He always charmed His listeners, but today there was a quiet tension, a breathless silence, as though the very trees and assembled animals were listening to the Pale One's softly spoken words.

Next, the tall chieftain slowly climbed the small mound and stood beside the Prophet. The two eagle feathers in the hair of the chieftain projected well above the head of the Healer. Suddenly, a miracle happened.

"Before anyone else saw the sunlight," the legend declares, "a golden shaft of radiant beauty came down from some clouds banked high with fire-light and touched the curling hair of the Prophet, diffusing itself like a halo, until He stood, a luminous creature, painting all the ground around Him with gold. The people then fell down, saying, 'Behold, He is indeed the Dawn God who has come to walk among us!' and 'He draws His power from the Star of the Dawning.'"

The tall chieftain, seeing the Great One clothed in gold light, knelt in the dust beside Him and laid his cheek on the hem of the Prophet's mantle.

The Seneca tribesman who told Hansen the legend tells her that "All nations know He was of the Dawn Star, and that is why, even now, no nation of the ancient people known as 'red-skins' will ever make war or fight a battle while the Sacred Star of Peace is still shining in the great heavens. They dare not, for it is the Star of the Prophet."

Hansen notes that she heard this story from a Senecan named Big Tree but had lost contact with him over the years.

"He once told this legend to a child to illustrate the fact that the tallest men are not always the greatest," Hansen writes. "I hope he will not mind its inclusion here."

She also points out that the story is a variation on another recorded by historian Hubert Bancroft, so she believes the legend is authentic to Seneca tradition.

The Truth of the Pale God Is Preserved

In a chapter called "The O'Chippewa Council," Hansen inserts herself as a character in the story told in "He Walked The Americas," though she refers to herself with male pronouns, keeping up the subterfuge that she would maintain for many years. She speaks of meeting a kindly chief called Dark Thunder in a forest of what we now call Michigan.

"Toward him came the college student," Hansen writes, referring to herself, "the one the tribe adopted by 'blood rites' and for whom there was warm affection. That affection was more than mutual. That child of the white race found all of these people charming. He admired the agile and catlike grace of the dancers; the smooth silken skin of the women; the quiet beauty of their language, at times most hauntingly poetic in its phrasing. They lived in a world unknown to white men, a world in which the past was present; a past more distant than our histories.

"Upon their reservations," Hansen continues, "poverty-stricken and spirit-broken, the student was learning to see them through their own eyes – as the Ancient Ones and keepers of the Olden Knowledge. Theirs was a very rigid culture with patterns that ran back to antique cities old before the rise of Egypt."

Next, an interesting dialogue began between Hansen as a "he" and Dark Thunder as the tribal leader blew his pipe smoke to the four directions.

"My father," Hansen asked, "why are you blowing the smoke rings?"

Dark Thunder finished his meditation before answering, "Because if you look across the water which rolls from the Bay we call Kee-weenah, you will see it is touched with sun-fire."

"Yes," young Hansen forthrightly replied, "that comes from the clouds of scarlet which the sun paints as he leaves us to light the lands beyond the horizon."

"You learn well in the schools of the White Man," Dark Thunder responded.

"You hint that there is another meaning?" Hansen wondered aloud.

At which point Dark Thunder spoke of the Pale God.

"Long ago," he said, "there came to us a Prophet. He asked each tribe to name Him, for to Him names were nothing. So we called Him Wis-ah-co, and we covered His paths with flowers so that He always walked on petals. Now he does the same for the spirits who leave us and I was giving Wah-tay-see my blessing."

"Yes, I heard of her death this morning; a lovely young girl, her cheeks bright with fever . . ."

"The coughing-sickness of the White Man. Once such diseases were unknown among us, but something in our blood seems to invite them," Dark Thunder said.

Hansen offered "his" opinion, saying, "Perhaps in the blood of White Man is a substance which resists them, having been built up through the ages. Yet the blood of Red Man, having never coped with these diseases, does not have this resistance."

"Perhaps," Dark Thunder answered.

"But tell me of this Prophet," Hansen prodded. "What was He like? Where did He come from?"

"Your desire for knowledge is a thirst never-ending," the old one replied.

"Forgive me if I am too inquisitive," Hansen said apologetically, "but I have never glimpsed this knowledge and my time here is short. A summer vacation is of such short duration to grasp even a fragment of it."

We see here in Hansen's part of the conversation that she/he is a truly humble student, eager to sit at the feet of her Native-American teachers and drink in everything she can be taught. There is not the slightest trace of a self-entitled, "white" condescension, no sense of superiority, social or cultural. Hansen wants to see the legends she hears from within the indigenous cultures, to become a native herself and not be merely an intrusive "other" recording the stories of primitive "inferiors." This was not always the case in 20th century anthropology and we restate that Hansen was in many ways ahead of her time as she went about her fieldwork.

"Very well," Dark Thunder said, "let us speak of the Prophet. He was bearded and pale of feature – without doubt a White Man. He came to us one day at dawning and the light touched His hair with the sheen of red-gold until it shone like newly-mined copper. Yet He was not as the men of your people. This one was a god, with high soul-stature. If He touched a man who was wounded, that one became healed.

"His robe was long and white, down to the hemline, which almost hid His

THE SEARCH FOR THE "PALE PROPHET" IN ANCIENT AMERICA

golden sandals" the old man continued. "Everyone wished to make Him white robes, for then He would leave behind the old ones, and all that He touched was enchanted with His godlike power of healing."

"Why do you call Him the Prophet?" young Hansen asked.

"Because He not only walked among us, He also walked the realms of the future."

"Are you sure that He was not one of the Black Robes who came to this land with Columbus?"

"I am sure," Dark Thunder said. "He came to us when we had cities, more than a thousand winters before the days of the Black Robes and the Long Knives."

"What a strange legend," Hansen said.

"You do not believe what I am saying," Dark Thunder said. "You think I speak to you with a forked tongue."

Hansen assured the old man she did not think he intended to deceive her/him and that she/he wanted to write these stories down.

"Just to spread them among the White Man?" Dark Thunder asked. "So that he can laugh at us and speak lightly of things about which he knows nothing?"

"No. Someday, I must make a book of such stories," Hansen said, "not for the amusement of White Man but for the teaching of your grandchildren's children beyond our time – many generations. Already there are few who can tell these stories. Are there any others around here that know them?"

Dark Thunder told her/him that such another such teacher would have to come from a far distance. Then he paid Hansen a great compliment.

"My child," he said, "you speak with the tongue of the Red Man, and knowledge beyond your number of winters shines from your words. Once we had books and priests to read them, but those were times long distant in the past. Books are of stuff that can be swept to oblivion. Since then, we have placed our stories in the chants of our people, but now even these are being forgotten. Your oldest books to us are but of yesterday, and how long may last these papers of your people? Yet, you are right. The chants are dying. I too would like to reach other tribes of our people and share with them our ancient history."

In due time came the night of the chanting, Hansen reports, and many sages were gathered, proud old men of noble bearing and speaking in different languages. Their names have been forgotten, but never the drama of their movements and the melodic poetry of their phrases.

An old warrior named Marksman, presumably the teacher who had come from a far land, rose to speak to the assembled. Although in years he was nearly eighty, his figure had the lynx-like grace of a young man, his long, neatly-braided hair still had the sheen of the blackbird, his teeth still as white as his grandson's

THE SEARCH FOR THE "PALE PROPHET" IN ANCIENT AMERICA

and his eyes still keen and alert.

"It is well tonight that we speak of the Pale God," Marksman began, "and fitting as well that we council with others, greeting our enemies as brothers, for such would have been the wish of the Prophet. I have heard some talk among the lodges that the Lord of Wind and Water was but a myth brought down by the old ones from times beyond our present reckoning. That is true, but what a strange legend! If the youth among our people doubt the wide-flung strength of this ancient story, look about at His symbols from tribe to tribe across the Broad Land."

Marksman began to recount various sacred traditions that showed the people's reverence for the Pale God, such as the ceremonial smoking of tobacco mixed with cedar when they were returning from the war trail.

"Is it not to ask His forgiveness, as was once taught by the Pale God?" he asked rhetorically. "Why do we plant these trees upon the Great Mounds – these ancient histories of our cities? Was it not to warn all men that once He walked here; the Sacred One, the Miracle Worker? And the color of snow; among all nations it stands for peace. Why is this so? Because He wore it. From nation to nation, He taught the people to live in peace and to speak in council, thus settling all their problems. This was His way and the way of His Father. Why do we raise our hands up in greeting? Because that was His peace sign, a tradition which we still follow."

Marksman went on to describe how the Prophet had used the cross as another sacred symbol, which He wore on the Hem of his garment as well as etched onto His two healing hands.

The strange custom of the Sun Dance is also proof of the Pale One, according to Marksman.

"How many here have ever seen the Sun Dance?" Marksman queried his listeners. "I know that our brothers, the Cheyenne and Dakotah, probably bear its scars on their bodies. Let us consider for a moment this strange dance: a self-torturing agony of suffering as danced by the young men.

"The ancient ones have told us that once this was a flying dance about a high pole, and that it came from the Old Red Land now forlornly sunken for many ages below the green waves of the ocean. [An allusion to Ancient Atlantis?] Perhaps it once belonged to the Wind God, which the Serpents made a dance of sacrifice in the times long vanished, many cycles before the Prophet's coming."

The Prophet, we learn, took the dance and made it a dance of "penance," Marksman said.

"Today," the aged Marksman went on, "as a sacrifice for their people, the young men allow the thongs from the tall pole to be tied under a two-finger-wide strip by opening the skin of each breast, then dancing night and day for four days until they drop and are again freed from the suffering of the Sun Dance. Is it not strange that we hang our young men thus in pain from a dead tree? I know not why, but we feel that a blessing or a righting of wrong is certain to follow."

While it may seem bizarre to our ways of thinking, the Native American ceremony of hanging young men from a dead tree as part of a ritual of repentance is very reminiscent of the crucifixion of Jesus, who willingly endured the agonies of execution on a wooden cross as a "blessing" and "to right that which was wrong."

"Our tribe no longer dances the Sun Dance," Marksman said, "but we still remember the Prophet. In the Wisacoo Lodge and many others there are some who still know His secret language, but those things are being fast forgotten."

"He left us," Marksman concludes, "and to Him I raise the Peace Pipe, the tobacco mixed with cedar shavings, and blow the smoke to the four directions, thus making the sign of His cross."

THE SEARCH FOR THE "PALE PROPHET" IN ANCIENT AMERICA

DR. L.B.S. LEAKEY, famed anthropologist, REPORTS DISCOVERIES IN THE GREAT RIFT VALLEY OF AFRICA INDICATING THAT THE ANCIENT BEACHES UNCOVERED IN 1926 CORRESPOND TO THE WORLD FLOOD CYCLES.

ACCORDING TO MODERN SCIENTISTS, THE PRIMITIVE AFRICAN BUSHMAN PRESENTS THE GREATEST OF ALL ANTHROPOLOGICAL RIDDLES. HIS BRAIN CAPACITY IS BETTER THAN THE AVERAGE OF ANY LIVING RACE.

ON THE FIRST BEACH, LEAKEY AND HIS CO-WORKERS UNCOVERED BURIALS OF A REMOTE RACIAL TYPE – CERTAINLY NOT NEGROID. BEAUTIFULLY DECORATED POTTERY, BEADS and FLINT MORTARS FOR CRUSHING GRAIN, INDICATED THEY WERE A PEOPLE of CULTURE.

The Pale Prophet Strikes Water and Hansen Speaks to the Snake Priest

Along the trail to the sunset the Pale Prophet walked. No tribe was too remote for His sacred visits, none too poor for His ministrations, none too warlike for His councils. If He heard of a war, He went there, called the chieftains into conclave, divided up the territory, gave them seeds and taught them gardening.

"Do not kill," the Pale One told them, "unless you are hungry, and then ask the animal's forgiveness and explain your great need to him before you ever pull the bowstring."

Hansen notes that this is a rule that no Native American would be so rash as to violate. So before going out to hunt, the tribes would hold a ritual of prayer and dance.

NAMING A FUTURE CITY IN WASHINGTON

To the Chinooks, the Prophet came. Once, when leaning on His long staff, He pointed down to the plain below them. He told them He could see a future time when a city would be spread out across the now empty plain, a city of the White Man called "Tacoma." "Tacoma" is a variation on a name of the Pale One, "Tla-acomah," which means "Lord Miracle Worker."

WATER FROM A ROCK

The Healer came to the land of the Havasu one early dawn; they saw He of the White Robe coming.

"The flame of dawn touched His golden sandals," Hansen writes, "and long before they saw Him raise one arm in greeting, meaning Peace and Prosperity to You, they whispered to one another: 'He comes to us! The Great Tacobya! The mighty Master Miracle Worker!'"

Then, with the whole tribe watching, He stopped and tapped a large rock in the midst of the dry desert with his long staff and there gushed forth water. He stooped and drank from the sacred water, which is still called the Spring of Tacobya.

There is a similar moment in Exodus, Chapter 17. Moses is leading the Israelites through the desert when they begin to complain they have nothing to drink. At which point Moses asks, "Why do you find fault with me? Why do you put the Lord to the proof?" But the people still thirst, and Moses responds to their continued murmuring by crying out to the Lord. The Lord then instructs Moses to strike a certain rock with the same rod with which Moses had struck the Nile. Water comes out of the rock and the people are able to drink. Moses names the location after the faultfinding of Israel, who had said, "Is the Lord among us or not?"

FORSAKING ALL WARFARE

The Prophet came to the people of the White Rock, who told Him that they had come there after the Great War in the Southland, where all their cities were left burning and they were reduced to a splinter of their once mighty power. With much sadness and continual homesickness, they remembered their disaster. The legends say the Prophet told them of another nation which had to flee oppression in days long-vanished, a probable reference to the sojourn of the Israelites out of Egypt.

The Prophet then showed the people of the White Rock the beauty of their new land and how to make their gardens prosper. When He told the people He was leaving, they were again desolate with sadness.

"Heavy our hearts," they told Him, "and dark our future on that day when you will leave us, for there are tribes westward known to men as the Sacrificers. Some day they will overwhelm us."

"Then unto these Serpent People I will go," the Master replied, "and I will teach them."

"Yea," they answered, "but will nevermore we see you?"

"In truth," the Pale One said, "I give to you a promise. Keep you my precepts, forsake all warfare, and you shall have my blessing even beyond the White Man's coming. And woe to the hands that are raised against you."

But still the people pressed Him about returning. Will He ever come back?

"Yea, if to my teaching you are faithful," he said, "and to show that you have lived each day rightly, leave a light at night burning against the time I will return through the Dawn Light, and lead thee unto My Father's Kingdom."

So every night, Hansen writes, a light is burning among these tribes that we call "heathen."

THE SEARCH FOR THE "PALE PROPHET" IN ANCIENT AMERICA

HANSEN'S DIALOGUE WITH THE SNAKE PRIEST

Hansen writes of her own 20th century encounter with the Snake Priest of the Hopi tribe of Arizona. She came bearing a gift, a condor feather, which she had obtained at a White Man's zoo.

"Thank you for the condor feather," the Snake Priest said. "For us, it is a bird of legend."

"It is that for all the tribes of the American Indian people," she answered him.

Hansen describes his beautiful clothes and observes his relatively light skin and utterly beardless face. She stood for a while in silence, because "to speak too soon or abruptly would prove only that one had little breeding in the quiet ceremonious world of the Red Man."

"You wrote to me in your letter," the Snake Priest said, "that you wished to speak to me of the Pale God? Of those days now, few men remember."

"That I have learned," young Hansen affirmed. "Yet I would put those days in a book for reading so that young Red Men will remember the Ancients, the heritage of all you people."

"Perhaps in your book," the Snake Priest said, "you will write of my people; of their kindness, their old traditions, their peaceful ways and their love of beauty. We belong here on the desert."

Hansen murmured, "It is a wild land."

"It is our land," the Snake Priest countered, "and without it, life would not be worth living."

"Ah, yes," she said. "The desert has a strange fascination."

"It is easy out here to believe in the Fire God," he said. "Look at those mountainous shafts of red rock, torn and shattered and twisted upward. Here is a strange sort of soul-magic; a land of weird fascination."

"A never-never land of beauty?" she asked.

"I said it was easy to believe in the Fire God," the Snake Priest said. "See how he crushed and mauled the mountains? Then twisted them up. Even the water holes, cool and turquoise, are not always filled with good water. You can tell by looking for animal skeletons."

The awe with which the Snake Priest regards the twisted rocks is echoed in Ecclesiastes, Chapter 7, verse 13: "Consider the work of God; who can make straight what He has made crooked?"

"You should not have come to us in summer," the Snake Priest said. "It is not the time to speak of the Ancients, but there are some hints that I can give you. It is well that you move among the Nations. Ask the High Priest in winter. Perhaps he will not turn his back upon you, if he believes that you are honest and do not come to make fun of the stories. And when you yourself walk the Broad Land, remember that He was here before you. Learn to see His sign when it is carved in the canyons. Learn to know His name when you hear it spoken."

The Snake Priest further counseled Hansen to remember that the Pale Prophet had loved the beauty of the desert when she went forth to speak to the people of the Healer.

"Speak of this," he advised, "when you talk to the people and they will open their hearts to you when they see that your path of life is not crooked but open and filled with beauty. They will speak and send you away with a blessing: 'May the Great Spirit walk with you down a life path of beauty.' Speak of this and you speak of the Prophet. Speak like this and you will hear of the Prophet."

This is a fascinating glimpse into Hansen's skills working in the field as an anthropologist. She is able to inspire trust in the Snake Priest by not trampling upon his dignity or his manners and mores. Her genuine respect for the ancient stories of the Pale Prophet is clearly evident and there are even hints that her own spiritual quest is beginning, a quest separate from her research into the Native Americans' culture. Hansen may come to revere the Healer in personal terms, as though she has stumbled on to her own salvation in a manner similar to the indigenous peoples she writes about. The loving hands of the Bearded One reach out to her through the millennia as well, and she is just as moved by His grace.

THE LIVING MEMORY OF THE MASTER

Hansen writes: "Perhaps to no tribe is the memory of the Master more a living thing than it is with the Seri; the shaggy-haired, neglected Seri, living in poverty-stricken squalor upon Mexico's Triburon Island. Still ruled by their sacrificing priesthood are the hardy untamed Seri; still painting their cheeks with the ancient totem.

"Thousands of years ago, say the Chanters, the Seri were part of the Serpent People, living together with the Turtles in their powerful ocean homeland, long before the time of the Deluge. After the great disaster, they fled to the land called the Snows of the Southland. Here they built giant cities and called themselves the Men of the Mountains. Underneath their powerful cities were the giant caverns of the serpent. After many ages, a northern army came down and burned those cities, and then the Serpents fled through the caverns to where their ships were waiting and took themselves on the seas to other coastlines in a series of long migrations."

Triburon Island, the home of the Seri in the time Hansen was writing, is located in the Gulf of California.

The Master came to their people in a canoe powered by the wind. He stepped out on the beach in the early dawn. The people marveled at His long

THE SEARCH FOR THE "PALE PROPHET" IN ANCIENT AMERICA

white toga, His hair and beard gleaming with red lights, and His eyes the color of deep-sea water. They thought of Him as a beautiful teacher who suddenly took on the halo of godhood.

A man rushed out and fell before Him, crying: "Ahunt Azoma, Lord Miracle Worker, for you strange rumors have come to us. Heal these eyes for so long darkened. Bring back my sight of the trees and flowers, of the sea and the people all about me!"

The Master, stooping quickly, gathered in His hands some wet sand, placed it over the eyelids of the sightless man and said, "Go thee out and bathe in the ocean."

The Seri gathered about in breathless awe, waiting to see the outcome. If he who had been blinded came back to them seeing, then indeed a god was among them. If not, then there would be a sacrifice for the Snake God.

"The blinded man gave a scream of anguish," the legend goes, "then a cry of unutterable joy, and came toward them running wildly."

Sobbing, the man fell at the feet of the Healer. The watching throng also fell down and worshipped, saying, "Ahunt Azoma – Lord Miracle Worker."

For a long time the Master stayed with them, teaching them to store water in their giant, clay-baked pots. He taught them to feed their children who had been weaned so that fewer toddlers died. He showed them wild plants that could be prepared for cooking.

Prior to the Pale One's coming, the tribe controlled its population so that it would not overrun the island or deplete the food supply by allowing no children life beyond that number which the death of the aged provided. This ancient law was broken by the Master because it ran counter to the law He gave them: "Raise not the knife in bloody slaughter."

When it came time for the Prophet to leave, He called the Seri to sit in council.

"I am leaving you prosperous and happy," He said, "but other tribes need me, so I go to Papago."

"Nay, Lord, go not to Papago. They are an enemy tribe of wicked people."

But the Master smiled and said, "In My Father's Land are many lodges."

"Then tell us, Great Ahunt Azoma: You speak often of this Land of thy Father, yet you say not where it lies or in what direction."

Softly, the Bearded One gave His answer: "My Father's Land lies deep within you."

Many will recognize this as a restatement of Luke, Chapter 17, verses 20-21: "The kingdom of God is not coming with signs to be observed; nor will they say,

THE SEARCH FOR THE "PALE PROPHET" IN ANCIENT AMERICA

'Lo, here it is!' or 'There!' For behold, the kingdom of God is in the midst of you."

It is these wonderful consistencies between the Gospels we are familiar with and the heretofore little known legends gathered by Hansen that make her work among the Native Americans resonate so powerfully.

An Assassination Attempt on the Messenger of Peace

True to His word, the Pale Prophet next journeyed to the village of Papago and a people that the Seri had denounced to Him as their wicked enemies. The children had been playing noisily, and when the Lord of Wind and Water, whom the Papago call "E-see-cotl," was seen approaching, the people were embarrassed and roundly rebuked the young ones.

"Nay," said the Prophet to them in Papago. "Do not scold the little children, but instead let them come to me, for such is the will of My Father in Heaven."

This is easily cross-referenced with Matthew, Chapter 19, verses 13-14: "Then the children were brought to him that he might lay his hands on them and pray. The disciples rebuked the people, but Jesus said, 'Let the children come to me and do not hinder them; for to such belongs the kingdom of heaven.'"

When one is a child being raised in the Christian faith, the idea that Jesus has a special regard for children is one of the most basic tenets of a Sunday school education. The fact that this same idea carries over to the Lord of Wind and Water should not be a surprise.

As the Papago legend goes, the Prophet met and talked with the children every day. The Prophet did not live among the people but made His home on a distant mountain called Bavo-kee-vulick.

One day the Pale One wandered into a secret temple where a child was being sacrificed. In a red-hot anger, He snatched up the baby, healed its wounds, and, calling it by name, "gave it back its breathing."

The priesthood stared with their arms frozen. They were paralyzed and could not move, much as they would have liked to kill Him. The Master stepped outside where the people had gathered and He told them of the secret ceremony and that it was against all His teachings. The people were ashamed but still they feared the priesthood.

"That night," Hansen writes, "two priests determined to murder this saintly man who was winning the people. They stole out in the moonlight for Bavo-kee-vulick, slipping knives under their blankets. The moon was still up, yet the dawn light was coming as they neared the mountain."

The Prophet was kneeling in prayer in His cave as the assassins approached. Then He arose and waited their coming. As the two priests stood hidden just outside the cave, brandishing their knives, the Pale One stepped out to meet them.

"Why do you not step forth and kill me?" the Master challenged them. "I have no knife or rod to strike you. Yet you cannot, even though in the moonlight I stand revealed? Know you not that you cannot kill me until the tasks which were assigned by My Father to me upon this earth are finished?"

The earth suddenly began to tremble with a deafening roar. The rocks fell downward like rain, and "with the roar of a hundred oceans the mountain collapsed, leaving the Healer standing still on the rock in the moonlight."

The Pale One heard two voices pleading for Him to go to the village and tell the people how the mountain had entombed them. As the dawn light came, E-see-Cotl walked into the village. All the people stared in frightened awe at the mountain and then at the Prophet.

"Where are the priests," they asked, "who came to see you when the Fire God shook the mountain?"

"They came with knives before trembling," the Master answered. "They are still within the mountain, and from a great distance you can hear their voices. My Father has spoken in the earthquake. No more am I to live among you."

"Walking away from them in the dawn light went white-robed E-see-Cotl, nor ever after did they see Him," Hansen writes.

In these legends of the Prophet, it is rare for Him to leave a village or city without blessing the inhabitants and promising to return and take them to His Heavenly Home. Perhaps the Seri were right that their enemies in Papago were irredeemably wicked.

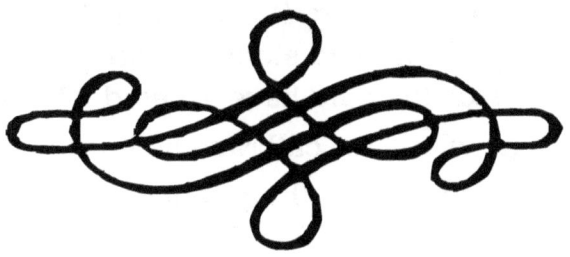

The Master's Authority

The Pale Prophet's traveling took Him to a tribe called the Dene, known today as the Navaho and Apaches, but at the time a lost tribe of the wandering Serpents. They met the Prophet in the wild red lands of Monument Valley.

The people here were skeptical of the Miracle Worker and the fantastic power He was rumored to command as the Lord of Wind and Water. The Dene questioned His right to that title.

"Is the power of this One God, whom you call Father, greater than that of the Fire God?" they asked. "His name no man breathes aloud, or the earth will begin shaking and the hot rocks burst from the volcanoes. The Fire God ever devours his children even as he destroyed our homeland."

Jesus is put to the test in a similar manner in the Gospels. As the story is told in Mark, Chapter 11, verses 28 and 29: "And the chief priests said to him, 'By what authority are you doing these things, or who gave you the authority to do them?' Jesus said to them, 'I will ask you a question; answer me, and I will tell you by what authority I do these things. Was the baptism of John from heaven or from men? Answer me.' And they argued with one another. 'If we say, "from heaven," he will say, "Why then did you not believe him?" But shall we say, "From men?"' They were afraid of the people, for all held that John was a real prophet. So they answered, 'We do not know.' And Jesus said to them, 'Neither will I tell you by what authority I do these things.'"

In a likewise way, the Dene are asking for some way of naming the God the Master serves in the hope of proving Him a charlatan. But the Pale One deigns to answer the Dene, which He had not done for the cunning Pharisees.

"My Father is a spirit who has no image. His power is greater than any other. Watch!" said the Prophet, pointing upward.

THE SEARCH FOR THE "PALE PROPHET" IN ANCIENT AMERICA

A giant rock which had been lying near them, half the size of a fallen cliff face, began to rise slowly above them. The Dene watched, eyes wide with terror, as it swayed and rose like a living thing. Had it fallen, it would have crushed them. Yet it straightened itself up slowly and stood upended on another rock, rocking gently and slowly, so that a child could have swayed it back and forward.

That part of the Dene whom we call Navaho have another legend.

To the Prophet, names meant nothing, but they are important to the Dene. So they asked the Healer the name of His One God. The Prophet asked them to name Him themselves, but they refused, saying that they knew not what name to give Him. [Echoing the "We do not know" reply of the Pharisees in the story above.]

The Dene then made a suggestion: "Surely in your childhood, across the ocean, you were told His name? What name did they tell you?"

So the Navaho have the name He gave them: Great Yeh-ho-vah.

"Today," writes Hansen, "White Man, hearing, is deeply puzzled."

Puzzled the White Man may be, but there is an undeniable phonetic linkage between the name "Jehovah" and the tribal name "Navaho." The clear intent of the Navaho was to call themselves a name that would translate as the "people of the One God," and their faith in what the Master told them about the name of His Father has carried down through the millennia, though its sacred origins may be at least partially lost in history. It only needed Hansen to come along and make its meaning apparent in our time.

The Pale Prophet Departs the Americas

L. Taylor Hansen writes of many more miracles and healings by the Pale One, of counseling the natives to choose the ways of peace over the ways of warfare, more wondrous moments than can fit in the present book. When she tells of the Pale Prophet's inevitable departure from the Americas, of His leaving by way of the Island of Cosmul in the Yucatan, she movingly relates the people's grief as they said goodbye.

"From far away arose a strange new sighing," Hansen writes, "borne on the wind from afar off, like the torrent of distant river. The people who had been waiting looked into each other's eyes and nodded, 'This is the day of His departure.'"

Closer came the lamentations, like the surge of a flood onrushing, and waves of people choked the highway. There was heard the weeping and wailing and mournful cries of untold thousands, jostling each other for a better view. But the loudest lamenting was still in the distance, from among the approaching priests and great men clad in their finest clothes. Next came the "bearded strangers," the chosen ones of the Master, who smiled and bowed as they passed.

Then the Holy One could be seen, carried on a litter and hailed as the Feathered Serpent. Clothed in a white robe of spotless silk, with the wide golden scarf of Mayan High Priest wrapped about Him above the waistline, His face was sad as He beheld the people. In an unending stream of blessings, the silent figure of the Pale God passed.

When He reached the vessel he would be leaving on, He turned and faced the crowds, "and never before or since, in all the Broad Land, was ever heard such a terrible silence. Sadly, the people fastened their eyes upon Him, knowing this was goodbye forever; trying to remember each tiny detail so they could tell their children's children, to be passed onward through the ages."

THE SEARCH FOR THE "PALE PROPHET" IN ANCIENT AMERICA

THE INDIGENOUS LORD'S PRAYER

Someone in the crowd began chanting an olden chant that the Master had taught them, which became known as the Chant of the Cosmul.

"Almighty Father who created all mankind, and bound us here in this realm of service, open to us thy hand of mercy, that we may have shelter and food for our bodies.

"Oh, you who dwell in the golden sunshine, in the liquid silver which falls from the rain clouds, in the depths of the sea and the power of the windstorm, Our Father, Who art in heaven, most holy is thy word.

"Guide us, oh Father, through life's trail of hardships, deliver us from all that is evil, for thine is the power from the ice to the lava, and thine is the glory forever and ever."

One can easily see aspects that the chant has in common with the familiar Lord's Prayer that Jesus taught his followers in the Gospels. It is essentially the same reverent sentiments but grounded in places to things familiar to the Prophet's indigenous audience in the Americas.

THE THUNDEROUS SOUND OF GRIEF

When the chant was concluded, the Pale One, still silent, raised His hands in benediction and farewell. The cries of the people "broke forth like terrible thunder," Hansen writes, as the ship rapidly moved to the horizon and was gone.

"No one ever again saw the Serpent vessel," Hansen writes. "Never again in all the Broad Land, among the many waiting nations, has been heard the tread of those golden sandals, nor seen the beloved face of 'Kate-Zahl,' the Prophet."

Just Who Was The Prophet?

Just who was the Pale Prophet who brought such good news and healing to the indigenous peoples of the Americas?

Hansen first addresses this issue by saying: "The identity of the Plumed Serpent, or the Lord-of-Wind-and-Water, was an argument which raged with considerable heat at the time of the Conquest. The Catholic Church, confronted with the facts which seem to point to an early Christian, suggested that He may have been St. Thomas. In fact, in Mexico, He was often called St. Quetzal-Coatl."

Hansen makes reference to one Lord Kingsborough, a 19th century son of the English aristocracy who was so fascinated by the magnetic figure of the Pale God that he mortgaged all of his holdings to fund his research and died miserably in a debtor's prison. According to Hansen, Kingsborough was still the world's greatest authority on the Prophet, but she had been unable to obtain any of his books, all long lost to history, which surely must contain a great deal of valuable knowledge of the First Century of the Americas.

In any case, Kingsborough did not accept the St. Thomas theory, pointing to the fact that such words and concepts as sin, the Trinity, virgin birth, winged-beings or angels, the use of the Ten Commandments, ceremonies of baptism and marriage vows, were found to be similarly spread throughout both American continents. Kingsborough was therefore inclined to look a little higher than St. Thomas, while other experts kept their silence.

As for Hansen herself, "It is the opinion of the present writer that Kate-Zahl must have been an Essene. Since the opening of the Dead Sea Scrolls, we have come to know a good deal about this religious order of which Jesus was supposed to have been a member. We know now that they favored a white toga-like garment, wore no covering on their heads and always spoke of God as 'My Father.'"

For those unfamiliar with the Essenes, they were a sect of Second Temple

THE SEARCH FOR THE "PALE PROPHET" IN ANCIENT AMERICA

Judaism that flourished from the 2nd century B.C. to the first century A.D. They were the smallest of the three major Jewish sects, which also included the Pharisees and the Sadducees. The Essenes were dedicated to asceticism, voluntary poverty and daily immersion. They have gained fame in modern times as the result of the discovery of the Dead Sea Scrolls, which are commonly believed to be the Essenes' library and consist in part of multiple copies of portions of the Hebrew Bible. Their customs included ritually bathing every morning, eating together after prayer, devoting themselves to charity and kindness, forbidding the expression of anger, and preserving the secrets of their faith while being very mindful of the names of the angels as recorded in their writings. The Essenes lived throughout Roman Judea but were primarily found in the Israeli desert near the northwestern shore of the Dead Sea, where the Dead Sea Scrolls were discovered in 1946.

Hansen bolsters her belief in the Essene theory by explaining that various tribes of Native Americans seem to recognize the word.

"I have been corrected several times in its pronunciation," she writes. "Finally, a Choctaw informed me that this was the name for the Wind God. Although the name may differ from tribe to tribe, he said it could be recognized by the long e sound repeated twice with a hissing in between. Therefore, this word should be Eessee-Nee."

Hansen writes that Dr. Peter H. Buck, the Curator of the Bishop Museum of Hawaii, meanwhile, was not surprised that Wako or Wakea, the Polynesian name for the Pale One, was also to be traced throughout the Americas. Numerous plants found in both regions had convinced him that there had been commerce between them in ancient times. His people had traveled everywhere in the Pacific by star-navigation and no distance was impossible for them. Which leads Hansen to fall back on Dr. Buck's description of the Fair God as a man who arrived in the company of other men who apparently wore Mediterranean-style clothing and sailed on ships of a Mediterranean type and whose origin was probably the Red Sea.

According to Dr. Buck, China and India had similar legends of visitations by the Fair Prophet called Wako, stories he collected from natives of those lands then living in Hawaii. A legend from Japan refers to a Wako-Yama mountain there – the last word being Japanese for mountain. Therefore Dr. Buck concluded that the ships which brought and left the Fair God had already toured the Orient, undoubtedly in His company.

But beyond the fact that he regarded Wako or Wakea as a real person who lived during the century of Jesus, Dr. Buck was unwilling even to hazard a guess as to the identity of the Prophet.

"Perhaps we should leave the question with the Mexican archeologists," Hansen writes, "who, when tossed this puzzle of antiquity, simply shrug their shoul-

THE SEARCH FOR THE "PALE PROPHET" IN ANCIENT AMERICA

ders and answer: 'According to the Dead Sea Scrolls, there was a very saintly man preceding Jesus by about a century. This holy man, an Essene, had no name except "The Master" or "The Great Teacher." He was crucified but was apparently saved by the Essenes who were in the crowd surrounding him. Scientists in England have suggested the Polynesian chants allow for an error of time – perhaps a century, plus or minus.' Quien sabe? Who knows?'"

While Hansen and the sources she trusts stop short of calling the Pale Prophet Jesus himself, it is my opinion that the Fair God's spoken words are an unmistakably authentic expression of the Jesus of the Gospels, resonating with the authority of God Almighty in a similar, almost identical way. Along with tenderly working miracles of healing and casting His scheming, violent enemies aside with terrifying acts of God, the Pale One moves through the landscape of the Americas with the grace of an indisputably holy entity of kindness and love.

There are similar stories of Jesus gracing India, China and Japan with his presence during what are called Jesus' "missing years" – the time between his visit at age twelve to the temple in Jerusalem and the beginning of his public ministry at age 30 – that only add to the likelihood of "He Walked The Americas," which Hansen wrote more than 50 years ago, being a true history of the Son of Man bringing the Good News of the Gospel to an entire world thirsting for righteousness and salvation.

Though, again, in the absence of proof, Hansen and the Mexican archeologists she quotes are correct in asking, "Who knows?"

Part Two

Selected Essays by L. Taylor Hansen from the pages of "Amazing Stories" and originally published in the 1940s.

THE SEARCH FOR THE "PALE PROPHET" IN ANCIENT AMERICA

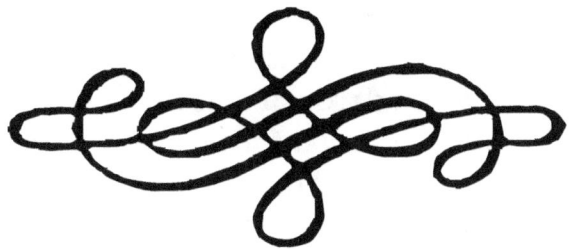

The following is an example of the "Scientific Mysteries" column that L. Taylor Hansen wrote in the 1940s for the pulp magazine "Amazing Stories." Here Hansen positions herself on the front lines of the battle against judging the races of the Earth by skin color. She even argues that African blacks are more recently and more highly evolved than the white race, though later experts have said there is no scientific basis for that assertion. One is surprised to discover that a tribe of Indians in Colombia semi-regularly produce white offspring with blond hair and that some of their indigenous language contains archaic Norse words. The 21st century reader should be prepared for words like "Negroid" and a discussion about the intelligence of a given race being a function of the shape of their skulls. The latter is another anthropological falsehood of her time that Hansen quickly dismisses.

The White Race—Does It Exist?
By L. Taylor Hansen

When we speak of the races of earth, is there really such a race as the white race? Is the color of a man's skin indicative of his origin?

There is no subject upon which more scientific nonsense, or rather let us say nonsense purporting to be science, has been written than upon the subject of race. The reason is not hard to find. Each man prefers his own type and considers his to be the highest. It is a subject which is more bound up with emotion than with reason, and the average man is still essentially an emotional animal.

Since the start of history, the question of a desirable racial type has run through as many fashions as women's clothes. The Germans, in preferring blonds, are not the first peoples to set a racial style. The Mayans admired slanting foreheads (and, strangely enough, their ironed-out foreheads, done in infancy, did not affect their intelligence), the Incas admired large ears, certain African tribes large lips, the Turks once admired excess fat and the Medieval artists thought excessively long necks were desirable.

The ideas of race which were popular during the days of our fathers are at present giving place to other standards of differentiation. If the tendency continues to its inevitable conclusion, we are going to discover that there is no such thing as a white race. For the standards of color by which our parents learned to classify mankind are far too superficial for the most advanced anthropologists. Today the scientists are busy pointing out that skeletal differences are far more important than the shade of the subject's skin.

Modern science regards the white, yellow, black, red and brown, even when the latter is eliminated or classified with the red as a subgroup under the yellow, with profound distrust. Thus the deeper structural differences are leading the foremost thinkers to suspect the old classifications so strongly that they are going out of fashion in any scientific discussions worthy of the name.

For example, Huntington contends that skin color is now distributed over the earth's surface according to the strength of the sun's rays and is only man's reaction to his environment. Dixon, of Harvard University, argues that all men are to be divided by skeletal differences into roundheads with narrow noses, roundheads with broad noses, long-heads with narrow noses, etc., completely ignoring hair texture and the color of the skin. Both of these eminent scientists have agreed that the Negro is not a primitive but a recently-evolved tropical type. In other words, a group of the long-heads, finding themselves in a tropical environment, evolved the spreading nostrils, thicker skull and blacker skin of the Negro. Thus the Negro is a late adaptation of Modern Man to a tropical environment.

Now it is interesting to note that mankind may be divided into two rather distinct types which are called "harmonics." One is a longheaded, long-faced individual with long eye-sockets. The hair in cross-section is inclined to be very oval, thus giving it a tendency to curl. The type is the Ancient Egyptian. Let us call him the "proto-Negroid" because, in its extremity, the type becomes more Negroid, the hair becoming exaggeratedly curly, etc. The Negro is a late branch from the type. In its earlier form, the skin is a tan shade and the eyes are long and deep-sunken, the nose delicate, the lips not too full. The stature is slight and slender. The hands and feet slender and delicate.

The "proto-Negroid" is sometimes called the "ancient longhead" and sometimes called the "Mediterranean Race." This latter name is somewhat incorrect, for though the people are to be found in the Mediterranean, they are centered in the area of the Indian Ocean. A better name for them would be the "Peoples of the Sea," for they are found upon every ancient shoreline.

In London, for example, when dredging for a new building, in the lowest basement, while digging in the gravels in which are to be found the remains of the Great English Channel forest which once covered that submerged valley, the human skulls which are brought up are the true type of the ancient longheaded "People of the Sea."

Again, in the channel islands of California, when the earliest skulls are unearthed, they are once more the harmonic longhead. A map of the cephalic index of living populations today would reveal that the longheads would live along the sea coasts, with the exception of the western coast of the Americas, where roundheads have displaced the ancient longheaded population.

The other "harmonic'" type is the round-headed, round-faced Asian with round eye-sockets and straight hair which is in the cross-section completely round. In the extremity this type develops the mongoloid eye-fold and becomes the typical Chinese.

These roundheads are concentrated most thickly in the region just north of the Himalayas. From here they pour in a thick stream from the Caspian into the Mediterranean and through Greece and Albania into Europe. Another arm runs northward through Russia into the Baltic while a third stream sweeps northeast across the Aleutian Islands and down the western coast of the Americas. Thus, from the map of present distribution, it is easy to see that the roundhead is an Asian and a landsman.

Now where does white man enter this picture?

Is he a cross? We learn with surprise that his is not a true or a harmonic type. Between the poles of the long-headed proto-Negroid and the round-headed Asian, in head form, shape of the face, eye-sockets and cross-section of the hair, varies that section of Modern Man which we designate as the "White Race." The variation is so profound that not only do we see all combinations within the same nationality but often within the same family group.

These facts force us to one of two conclusions. Either the white race is a very profound cross which has never remained in isolation long enough or inbred deeply enough to set its type, or it is the original stem from which the other two harmonics branched.

To meet these facts, some ingenious classifications have been offered. For example, there is Duckworth, who would make the roundheads the general type from which the longheads, making their way into the Indian Ocean and spreading from this point, were an early branch. However, that of Wissler* seems to be the most logical. He would make White Man and perhaps also the Polynesian Race the original stem. As he points out, the White Man is the most hairy of all the races and this is certainly a primitive characteristic.

[* Wissler, Clark, Curator of Anthropology, Amer. Museum of Nat. Hist., New York City. -Ed.]

THE SEARCH FOR THE "PALE PROPHET" IN ANCIENT AMERICA

When studying the very ancient nations, it is important for us to keep in mind the characteristic of facial hair. It is anthropological nonsense for us to classify the beardless Egyptians and Cretans as "'White Men." It would be more honest for us of the white race to admit that the first civilizations were not founded by men of our race but by the tan-skinned "Peoples of the Sea," some of whom, nevertheless, have contributed to the blood of the modern European.

As for this matter of superiority, the honors for Geniuses arc so evenly divided between the two harmonics that one could not truthfully give the palm to either the one type or the other. It would be a controversial question, for example, whether the round-headed Beethoven and Socrates were any greater than the long-headed Wagner and Shakespeare. And I would venture to wager that the honors in the prisons are just as evenly divided! Apparently, the only fair judge of potential intelligence is brain capacity in proportion to the frame, for much brain space is taken up in mere muscle control.

As for blondness, it is a stumbling block, for it is to be found in Northern Europe among both roundheads and longheads. Dixon suggests that there may be something about the food grown in this soil or some other physical reason which might contribute to fair hair and pale skin. However, the blonds to be found among the San Bias Indians of Colombia contradict this theory of Dixon. The Indians have their own names for their whites. Significantly, they are called "ya pisas" or "hairy ones." Sometimes they are nicknamed "moon children" in reference to the fact that white is the color sacred to the moon.

It is interesting to know that these blond Indians exist by the thousands. Some were taken to the Smithsonian Institute to be studied by the scientists. One of the most interesting facts to be discovered was that about one third of their words come from the ancient Norse. After realizing that these Indians did not have the white hair and pink eyes of the true albinos, but blue eyes and various shades of golden hair, the scientists decided that they were partial-albinos. One sage expressed the opinion that the San Bias tribe was in the process of changing its racial type and that the proceeding would have gone much further if an abnormal hatred for the conquering Spaniard had not caused the blonds to be placed under a marriage taboo.(This fact was attested to by the Indians themselves.)

The designation that the blonds were partial-albinos is an interesting one. The question which naturally arises is, if these people with their various shades of light hair and fair skin, are to be scientifically classified as partial-albinos, what are white Europeans? What is white man in general? Is he a partial-albino? Is white skin to be considered as various degrees of partial-albinism? And, if so, was this a general condition of the original stem along with a tendency to body-hair, from which diverging types acquired a more hairless skin and a deeper color? What do you think?

Another of Hansen's columns from "Amazing Stories." This one is an early example of her writings about the Pale Prophet, sometimes assumed to be Jesus Christ, visiting the indigenous people of the Americas. It is doubtful that Hansen realized she was sowing the first seeds of what would become her life's work, even her obsession, leading to what is, for many, her crowning achievement with "He Walked The Americas." Hansen went well beyond the "conventional wisdom" and documented a version of Christ who showed compassion and love to people far outside the borders of his native Israel and the literary confines of the Gospels.

The Bearded White Prophet
By L. Taylor Hansen

The amazing story of a great good man who taught the Aztecs the horror of blood sacrifices and ended them

Although Bancroft mentions Pidgeon's "Traditions of Decoodah" as one of the foremost authorities upon the Mound-Builders, one wonders if he ever read the book, as he seems to have missed its entire import. And this is strange for a man who devotes so much time and space to the minute descriptions of Sahu-gun on the historically less important horrors of Aztec ritual.

In the light of Decoodah's traditions, many bits of otherwise obscure legendary fragments, or stories gathered by the early travelers, take on an entirely different color. In the lore handed down among the Chippewa, the description of the beautiful city which they stormed and destroyed, upon the site of their present reservation on Lake Superior, and their subsequent intermarriage with the conquered women, gives one the needed sequel to Decoodah, as does the Legend of the Natchez. Both fill in parts of the structure whose outlines Decoodah has sketched.

THE SEARCH FOR THE "PALE PROPHET" IN ANCIENT AMERICA

Through Chippewa eyes, looking back down the vistas of their tribal memories, one sees a land of widely cultivated fields, of large decorated wooden pyramids with temple superstructures, and of rivers which served for highways of traffic. They are Mayan-like cities of wood instead of stone and they become links between the great wooden communal house of the Northwest and the Grecian beauty of the sculptured stonework of Mitla, Mexico.

Trying to fit this civilization of the Mississippi Valley into the composite picture of the Americas is not altogether impossible of fulfillment. When, in the time of King Quinnalpopoca, in Tenochtit-lan, "The City of the Lagoons," (Mexico City), a young noble by the name of Papaxtla inquired the direction of the silver and mother-of-pearl city of Ancient Tula, the priest of the Quetzal-god told him that there were four. One, said the priest, lay to the south in the Land-of-Thorns, one lay over the snow-capped mountains of the west in the Land-of-Flowers. One lay to the north in the Land-of-Cloud-Serpents, and one to the east over the Sunrise Sea.

Such an answer may have only been to put off * the youth's desire to see the city of story and song for himself. Could the people of Votan, who were the ones reported to have come from over the Sunrise Sea, have established so many other "Tulahs" after that dearly-remembered capital which they left behind? People from time immemorial have done just this. The world map is filled with "New England," "New Wales," "New York," "New Holland" and the like. Yet, of course, the answer may have been a lie.

Nevertheless, if it had been a lie, why would it have survived down to the present day? Why would the name of Land-of-Thorns be given to what was undoubtedly the Mayan country where self-torture by thorns was widely practiced according to their temple paintings? And, if it was not a lie, then the name of Cloud Serpents for the Mississippi is most significant, for Quetzalcoatl and Kul-kul-kan are the names* for the white-bearded prophet, The Great Reformer, who roamed from tribe to tribe, apparently from one end of the Americas to the other, preaching to each people in their native tongue and always decrying the twin evils of American Indian culture: war and human sacrifice. * Both mean "feathered serpent," 1st in Aztec, 2nd in Mayan.

So strong is the impression of this figure that we can almost date the location of a tribe by their legends of The Great White Reformer. For example, the Papagoes have been at their present location for two millennia because he is connected with their desert surroundings, although they have him confused with their earlier wind-god, while the Hopis are later migrants and do not connect the name of the White Reformer with their present surroundings. According to Mexican records, he left Mexico to go south in the year 64 A.D.

After the passing of The Great Reformer, the American Indian nations began to follow his religion. The new spiritual rebirth, and the worship of a supreme god, swept the old sacrificing priesthood into banishment. A period of great prosperity followed, in which, apparently, the main high priest took the name of the Great Reformer and was often confused in later records with the original prophet. In South America, this may have been the region of Vira-Cocha before the return of the Incas and their sun-worship; in Yucatan, it was during the reign of the Itzaes, who confused him with their own earlier deity; and in Mexico, it was during the reign of the Toltecs and the rise of Tula, The Magnificent, before the return of the Aztec ritual which was sacrifice run amuck.

Strangely enough, into this continent-wide picture, the Mounds offer evidence of the same Great Reformer. The open hand, the T-symbol and the cross which Quetzal-coatl took for his personal emblems are to be liberally found in the Mounds. Fragmentary legends of the Mississippi mention him, though he is often confused with the moon (because of his white color evidently) even as, farther west, the Algonquin confuse him with the elder Twin, the Zunis with a long-forgotten emperor, and the Havasupai and neighboring tribes of the Mohave with a creator-deity who survived the flood.

After years of great prosperity, the sacrificing priesthood came back into power. With the Itzaes, it may have been the Quiche invasion, or a new wave from the sacrificing Caribbean. With the Toltec, the end of the capital city of Tula and its golden age came probably with the invasion of the Chichimec, while in the Mississippi the counter-revolution in religion came with the invasion of the sacrificing Turtle and The Snake.

According to Decoodah, not all of the religious temples were places of sacrifice. In describing the mound which had always been the holy-of-holies of the Ancient Elks, Decoodah says that none but the sanctified foot of a high priest had ever trod upon that sacred spot, nor had it ever known death, violence, or even the shedding of blood until the coming of the white man. This is certain evidence of a religion other than that of the "Southerners," who burned the hearts of their enemies in their "Eternal Fire," or even the later religion of the Elks themselves, who sacrificed to both the sun and the moon.

We know from Mexican records that the Great White Reformer lived in a quiet garden in the north where he had taught many disciples to spread his doctrines before crossing the tall snow-capped mountains on his way to Cholula. Is it possible that this garden might have been in the Mississippi Valley?

Not only do we have much evidence in the Mounds of the presence of the White Reformer, but the symbol of the Plumed-Serpent, which was his symbol, runs from the Pueblos to the Sioux. Many young Indians have come to the present writer, puzzled by the evidence of what they have been taught to believe an exclusively Mexican religion, in the lore of their own tribe.

THE SEARCH FOR THE "PALE PROPHET" IN ANCIENT AMERICA

Little work has been done to correlate the civilizations of the Americas, but when it is finally done, this rather striking figure of The Great White Prophet, a little too romantic and imagination-seizing for science to regard as proper material for study, will be found to be a splendid date-stone.

The late inventor of good storage batteries, Mr. Willard,* used the wealth gained by his inventive genius to follow up his avocation, the study of The Mayans. In his book, "The Bearded Conqueror," he has confused two great American Indian figures, both white men. One was the earlier and much holier Prophet who always preached against sacrifice. The later one, The Bearded Conqueror, came into the Mayan Country at the head of an army and forced the custom of sacrifice back upon an unwilling populace. This latter figure, probably a thousand years later than the first in time, had, it is interesting to note, a black stick which hurled fire and killed at a distance. What white adventurer, probably wrecked or stranded, kept his musket and ammunition for such propitious moments that it would give him the command of an army and finally bring him the throne of the Mayans?

These two white men, preserved by the history and legends of a red man's world, could not have been more opposite, evidently, in temperament and ideals. And this is lucky for solving the historical sequence, for otherwise they would be bound to be confused by future students following in the footsteps of Mr. Willard. However, in spite of this confusion, the contribution of the inventor of our automobile battery to the better understanding of the "Bearded Conqueror" is most welcome.

One must add that there are other white men recorded by American Indian legend and history beside these two and the founders of Ancient Chan-Chan, who may have been early white men of the Spider Totem. There is Wako the Prophet of the South Seas, who may have been The Great White Prophet of North America. Also, there are the Lambayakas, who landed with their court just north of Chan-Chan, upon the Pacific Coast of South America; and there is the story preserved among the wild Seri of Lower California of the ship of seafaring Norsemen who carried powerful bows and arrows, who burned whale oil and whose most outstanding woman character on board, probably the wife of the ship's master, was a flaming red-head. These Norse described the homes they left behind in their own land, stayed an entire season, intermarried with some of the natives, and finally left, taking some natives with them and leaving some of their own members behind. The Seri will tell you that Norse blood is the reason that the Mayos have pale skin, blue eyes, and grow a beard, although they are apparently full-blooded Indians.*

Yet of all these occasional travelers, none are so universally-beloved and honored by all tribes, even though those tribes have long since returned to sacrifice, as the figure of the Great Reformer, or the White Prophet, as he is often called, who predicted the coming of the white man and who is still secretly worshipped by many American Indians who are nominally Christians.

*T. A. Willard of Willard Batteries. The great inventor died this year, and in his death, Mayan archaeology loses one of its most popular writers.

* The Mayo tribe is located upon the Mayo River near Yaqui and Seri territory. Cajeme was one of the white-skinned, blue-eyed, full-blooded Mayos. He became a great Yaqui chief, as politically the Mayo are a sub-tribe of the Yaqui. The author was acquainted with a full-blooded Mayo (at least as far as was known) who was red-haired and so fair that everyone guessed him to be either a Swede or an Irishman. People simply refused to believe that he was a Mexican Indian.

*Also confused by certain Mayan records, or traditions.

REFERENCES Willard, T. A.: The Bearded Conqueror (Kul-kulkan).

Willard, T. A.: The City of the Rain Well.

F. W. Hodge: Handbook of the American Indian.

Geo. Wharton James: Indians of the Painted Desert.

Washington Mathews: Navaho Legends.

Bancroft: Native Races (for interesting fads on the Mounds).

Bancroft: Native Races (for summary of Quet-zal-coatl legends).

For facts on The White Prophet in Yucatan see all discussions on Itzamul, his sacred city, by Central Amer. authorities and Bancroft for a summary of historical legends.

Personal research by author for historical legend of the Chippewas.

THE SEARCH FOR THE "PALE PROPHET" IN ANCIENT AMERICA

In this essay, Hansen deals with a subject close to the heart of many a student of myth and believers in the ancient astronauts approach to the UFO phenomenon, that being the universality of certain myths. That universal similarity points to a common source for most of mankind's beliefs in and subservience to gods from another world. In this particular instance, Hansen makes connections between ancient Egyptian and Native American gods even though those civilizations were worlds apart in many ways. Note also that Hansen references herself as a male in the last paragraph.

The Totem Of The Wolf
By L. Taylor Hansen

What is the answer to this totem's widespread distribution in both hemispheres of the earth?

The often indifferent, sometimes scornful, Apaches, are among the war-like American Indians; their prize fighting men are of The Totem of The Wolf. Like their cousins, the Navaho, whose language is still comprehensible, these Dene people are worshippers of several totems, showing a strong and ancient intermixture. Yet the Amen-figure of the Dragon, though prominent, is subservient to the powerful and mystic Coyote-Man. The Dene have often been accused of slavishly copying other rites, but this trilogy of culture comes all the way down with them from the far north.

The only seeming explanation is that The Dragon had already drenched the north with his culture to the Aleutian Bridge, and perhaps beyond, when The Wolf crossed over from Asia. These are the two totems in this trilogy the most easily accounted for, while that of The Great Fish, apparently already having yielded to the later Dragon, was to be found, at the time of the passage of The Wolf, spasmodically suggested by islanded groups and therefore, only spasmodically absorbed.

THE SEARCH FOR THE "PALE PROPHET" IN ANCIENT AMERICA

It is a most suggestive fact that not only in languages, but also in totems, the eastern part of the United States is more homogeneous than the Pacific Coast. In the eastern part of the country, we are dealing primarily with the Atlantic totems, while on the Pacific Coast, we find ourselves entangled not only with the large Pacific totems but also with partly absorbed or submerged Atlantic totems. This should help to demonstrate.

The Apaches, never numerous, produced two outstanding military geniuses, Cochise and Geronimo. The first resisted an act of stupid treachery by many years of successful warfare. He finally made peace as a victor and chose the location of his people's reservation. The latter, his nephew, resented the removal of his people to a lesser reservation despite treaty stipulations. With less than thirty warriors, often less than twenty, burdened by women and children, and outnumbered from three hundred to a thousand to one, they successfully defied both the armies of Mexico and the United States for over a decade until taken by treachery from their native Arizona.

The origin legend of The Klamath River Indians is typical. They will tell you that Ed-weech-me came west where he found that The Bear (The Pomo Tribe?) was ruling the land. The Bear thought that all he had to do was to look through his fingers at anyone and that person immediately died. (This being a ritualistic gesture of the sun dance, it should identify The Bear as Algonquin, if indeed, Decoodah had not already done so, and therefore underscores his identity.)

At that time, say the Klamath, the sons of The Bear were The Snakes, Two Eagles, and The Great Fish. Apparently then, The Bear had conquered and was ruling over these minor fragments of former people, when Ed-weech-me, definitely another name for The Elder or The Wind-god, came into the land. The latter hero defeated the minor peoples, thus reducing The Bear to impotence.

From this legend it appears that the Algonquin came west in two waves, the second wave of which included the Klamath. Yet from another legend we gain a still further glimpse into the past. The Shasta tell us that they once drove from the vicinity of that snowy peak a people who worshipped it as the home of The Deity where their sacred-fire dwelt. As we recognize again the Great Dragon, the Shasta tell us further that these people had great, square communal houses in which they held their dances, and once more we recognize the architecture of the Caribbean. To this story, the Modoc add that the Fire-god hid himself in Mt. Shasta because a great wind hit the land and he was afraid. He sent his daughter out to ask the wind to go away but she disobeyed his orders in some minor way and fell into the hands of The Bear as a prisoner. This should identify The Bear as either the army of The Wind, or an ally. In any case, The Bear was opposed to the Dragon, who shut himself up in his mountain fort.

A few facts seem to identify the role which The Wolf, or Coyote-Man, played

THE SEARCH FOR THE "PALE PROPHET" IN ANCIENT AMERICA

in this Dragon struggle. In the first place, nearly all of the legends give Coyote the credit for stealing the fire.

He usually has allies, it is true, but he is the main actor.

"The Popul Vuh," which is such a plain story of * the overthrow of the Votanic Empire that it would seem the main last act of the drama took place in Central America, has a most curious sequel in Central California. Among The Southern Sierra Miwok, Biurett has listed a legendary fragment which sounds like an echo of "The Popul Vuh." The main drama in which the battle between the hero Yayil and the ruler of a kingdom by the Southern Sea took place after the Great World Fire in which Falcon (evidently their totem) and his ally Coyote escaped the conflagration, along with Condor, like the famous book, was at the capital city of this Southern Kingdom.

The rulers also played a game, and the hero was defeated and then burned in their great fire. Then, like "The Popul Vuh," the son returned for a belated revenge. As in "The Popul Vuh," Owl had a prominent part as an ally of the Southern Power, and as in that book, the hero's son (Falcon to the Miwok, in the P.V. it was twin sons) and his great friend play the game once more and win. The rulers of the Southern Power are then burned in their own Great-fire. In connection with this legend, it is interesting that Yehl among the Thlinkeets is The Raven, and his home is in the East-wind, but he divides his power with The Wolf. The Thlinkeets dwell far up toward the Aleutian Bridge.

When the legends of the Apaches are studied, they should go a long way to clearing up obscure corners of this history, for apparently Coyote-man was one of the main characters of the Dragon War, as the Navahos say, and it was due to "The Twins," of whom Coyote, or Wolf, is The Younger, that the "Great Monsters who were devouring mankind," undoubtedly The Dragon, were finally defeated. More would be known of this early struggle if all tribes were studied as to their reverence for or abhorrence for twins.

Apache mythology is almost an unknown territory to science.

The author has discovered in personal contacts that the tribes revering twins are the ones who are most impressed by the Egyptian temple paintings, while the Pueblos are the best authorities upon the subject of costume. In order to receive a reaction of any kind, one must have a man thoroughly grounded in the lore of his tribe. Yet the Mayan and Quichua are as fascinated by the Egyptian likenesses as the Algonquin. Se-dulo, the rebellious Yaqui chief recently killed, was responsible for starting the present writer upon these investigations. I had studied these similarities between Egypt and among the Mayans back in the forest where the old priesthood still exists. It is one of the greatest of losses that this brilliant man should have thrown away years of unrecorded study when he became involved in typical intrigue and was killed in 1936.

THE SEARCH FOR THE "PALE PROPHET" IN ANCIENT AMERICA

Thus we would finally discover the lost Dragon fragments that were cut off from the Southern heart of the colossus by their Northern enemies.

Of one thing we are certain: that this struggle took place long before the rise of the Aztecs. Although they think of Quetzalcoatl (or Hua hua teotl) the "old, old god" as the original fire god, they worship particularly Tezcatlipoca who is a decided amalgamation of the Wolf with the mirror-holding sun cult of the Early Mississippi. And this in spite of the fact that their language connects them with the Nicaraos of Central America who, like the Aztecs, cremated their warriors in the Sacred-fire.

His war probably also took place long before the rise of The Great Reformer, for its western echoes show that it occurred as long ago in the west as it seems to have taken place in Central America.

One of the strangest things about the legend of The Twins, the Elder Wind deity, and the Younger Wolf, is the manner in which they spill over into Egypt. A Muskogean friend of the author, seeing a reproduction of the Egyptian temple painting in which Osiris is giving the bowl of life to the Pharaoh, while Set stands behind them, inquired with great interest as to the direction and origin of "the tribe who started that legend." Later, it became a game to take an Indian to where the print could be casually passed in an album of Mayan and other temple paintings and watch the manner in which they always lingered over it. Most of them agree that Set's costume is entirely correct, though they do not recognize his Egyptian name. Yet they exclaim that his correct color is black, though whether he originated it, or whether the Turtle did, is a matter of debate. Furthermore, they all identify Osiris as "The Elder Brother" or the "Breath-Master," though they insist the name should be pronounced O-see-rees in order to have the hissing sound and the ee-ee repetition.

What is the meaning behind the universality of this totem? Does it go back to pre-dynastic Egypt, to the very earliest vase ever to be dug from Egyptian territory, in which the pictured figures indulging in a hunt or a hunting dance wear a fox skin attached to their belts in exactly the same manner in which the Pueblos attach it today? Perhaps we will never know.

For all the antiquity of their totem, however, the Dene people were apparently the last language to cross the Aleutians from Asia, carrying a tongue so homogeneous today that it may have come as late as fifteen hundred years ago. Yet, in spite of the fact that the many tribes of the Dene or Tenneh cling to this name for themselves, and all are imbued with a great reverence for Coyote-man, no group, save those who speak the Uto-Aztecan tongue and those found upon the shores of the Caribbean, bear such a dear imprint of contact with the early culture of The Dragon.

The reason for this is that, apparently, the land which today belongs to The

THE SEARCH FOR THE "PALE PROPHET" IN ANCIENT AMERICA

Dene people of The Wolf was formerly wrested from The Dragon. The names of the mountains and other features of the land right up to the Aleutians and apparently beyond are definitely Dragon names. Thus we have the tribal names taken from these natural features among the peoples speaking the Dene or the Athapascan tongue, of "Ahtena," "Kaiyub-kho-tama," "Unak-ho-tana," "Nabesna-tana" as well as "Tanaina." and "Tanana" from the Upper and Lower Tanana, to mention a few. If one will trace the names of mountains into Asia, one will see that it did not stop at the Aleutians, this ancient power of the Sacred-fire to whom volcanoes are objects of worship.*

We cannot be certain what way the Dragon went. We can only be sure that the passage was previous to The Wolf, and that the conquered population was imbued deeply enough to influence the incoming wave. It is by the means of names that today we can trace the Gaels within what is English territory, and the Arymaras of South America within what was Quichua dominion when the Spanish first set foot upon the land.

Yet none of these names which The Dene carry is as antique and as suggestive of the Egyptian Amen as the name for the Apache fire-god who carries in his dances a flaming trident. His name, which is strictly taboo to mention, is Tamena. Such a startling bridge between the Egyptian Amen and the Mayan Zamna makes one wonder if the early Aztec name might have been Zamena or a contraction of "Aztec-Amen?"

Of course, the volcano-worshipping religion might have been spread by lava outpourings upon the coast, some of which are less than five hundred years old. The skeleton of a man as well as moccasins and a tepee abandoned in the hail of ashes from Crater Lake when it was an active volcano have been found. The lost villages of the Chumash may or may not have been older than this. Lavas are rather hard to date except by tree-growth.

Upon these old patterns came Coyote-Man, The Younger Twin, the Mischievous One, and taking the lesser animals for his allies, as well as the disinherited Wind-god, or The Elder Twin, he successfully slew the Great Earth Monster in a struggle which lasted for generations and which dyed the earth of the Western lands with blood. Then for his smaller allies, who had long been denied the privilege of having it, Coyote stole the Sacred-fire.

Today the scornful Apaches, who stare at the stranger through half-shut eyes, are only allowed two dances a year by our government. One of these they have chosen to celebrate the coming-of-age for their young women. The other one is the weird "Devil-Dance." Yet, as the student of Amerind lore watches the five exotic figures sway with their flaming tridents, and realizes that he is looking upon the henchmen of "Tamena," he cannot help but wonder if the Apaches chose this dance as the other one because millennia ago, possibly before the dawn of our history, they defeated the world colossus of The Dragon?

References

A. Barrett: Myths of the So. Sierra Miwoh, Univ. of Cal. Press.

Joaquin Miller's Life Among The Modocs.

Clarke Wissler: Indians of the United States.

Charles E. Scott: Indian Tales. N. F. Vanguard Press, 19Z9.

Bancroft: Native Races, Vol. HI.

Okas. S. Graves: Lore and Legends of the Klamath River Indians, 1929.

Volcanoes of the Medicine Lake. Highland, California, by Chas. A. Andersen, 17 of Calif. Geol. Bulletin, Vol. 2S No. 7.

* Particularly along the Medicine Lake rift, and its volcanoes.

Dr. Lawrence, U. of C. geologist, secured a skeleton which had been discovered in 1924, covered with the lava of Crater Lake when it bore the Indian name of Mazamak and was a volcano. Later Dr. L. H. Cressman, anthropologist, and Dr. Warren D. Smith, geologist, both of Univ. of Oregon, were called to Tuckers Flounce Rock Ranch, thirty-four miles from Medford by the discovery of a skeleton seated in a lava cave of only 36 inches in diameter. This find was near the site of the first discovery. Lee Vye Walker of Klamath Falls has in his possession moccasins and part of a tent retrieved from under a lava flow. These were found in the same vicinity.

THE SEARCH FOR THE "PALE PROPHET" IN ANCIENT AMERICA

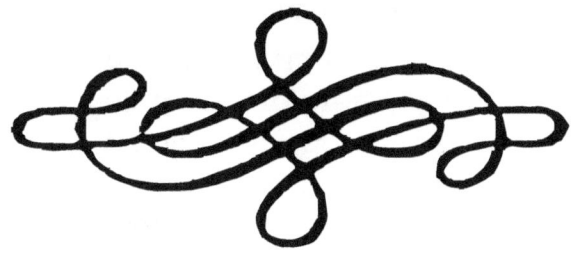

This essay is of particular interest since it begins with a flattering introduction by the editor of "Amazing Stories," Ray Palmer himself. Note that he refers to L. Taylor Hansen as "Mr. Hansen," abetting the deception she perpetrated for the most subversively feminist of reasons. Palmer explains his excitement at discovering corroboration of Raymond Shaver's "world underground" beliefs as well as the notion that the gods came from space to work their will upon the earth.

The Mystery Of Apache Tradition
The gods came from space and fought a great battle underground with the Red Fire Dragon
By L. Taylor Hansen

Followers of these articles by a scientist will be no more interested in this particular article than the followers of the Shaver Mystery, for here is scientific PROOF of the truth of Shaver's first story, "I Remember Lemuria!" This article, telling a newly discovered secret of the Apache, was rushed to us in haste by Mr. Hansen immediately upon his amazing discovery and was received BEFORE publication of Mr. Shaver's story. The reader will note that the Apache tradition just uncovered is actually the same story told by Shaver. Tiahuanaco IS one of the cities of ancient Mu, and Shaver's Titans DID come to make war on old Zeit in his underground stronghold and the Apache fled from their battle-ruined city and lost memory of its location until now!

Editor.

SINCE writing "The Totem of The Wolf," I have received the surprise of my life. That surprise was given me by the Apaches themselves. Along with all Amerind ethnologists, I had classified the Apache people as "Dene," or Athapascans.

THE SEARCH FOR THE "PALE PROPHET" IN ANCIENT AMERICA

They are completely Athapascan in language, and to the great Athapascan wash of languages running along the western part of the U. S. and Canada to the Aleutians, Coyote Man in his Wolf mask is usually the supreme spirit.

Furthermore, the Papagoes, Havasupai and others all designate the wild Apache as "Children of Coyote." Therefore, as up to the time of writing "The Totem of The Wolf," I had not had the opportunity of personally investigating the Apaches, I accepted the natural conclusion that they followed the traditions of other Athapascans in their culture. I now acknowledge that I was wrong. In fact, I was so astonishingly and completely wrong that I am still bewildered by what the Apaches themselves told me. Yet what they did tell me was so ancient and unexpectedly startling that I feel humbly grateful to them for lifting the veil a little from untold millenniums of history.

The haughty and scornful Mescallero Apaches, certainly the world's finest warriors, are neither interested in white men nor their ideas. They made that fact rather painfully clear when I first went among them. Yet their "Devil Dance" fascinated me as the most perfect example of the old Egyptian figure of Ammon-Ra extant in the modern world and it was inevitable that invited or not, I was going to witness his rites.

How he happened to be worshipped by an Athapascan-speaking (the group conceded to have been the last migrants from Asia, probably from the time-separation of the tongues, a two-thousand-year-old wave) tribe I had no idea. From the traditions of other Athapascans, they should have been his conquerors. At any rate, I invited myself to the reservation of the once-feared Mescalleros, and talked to the relatives of mighty Cochise and the descendants of Geronimo.

I had not come unprepared. However, I bided my time when seeking the man to question. The one who would know the traditions would be a main participant in the "Devil Dance." It would be useless to question anyone, perhaps a nobody.

The dance in itself was weird in the extreme. The girls who were to be initiated into the tribe had been praying and fasting for days, and now all dressed in white deerskin beaded garments of priceless beauty they awaited the coming of "The Men of the Mountains." The stars, the fitful light of the "Sacred Fire" and the throb of the tom-toms all joined to make the scene one to be etched on one's memory forever. A stir of expectancy among the blanket-clothed spectators, and the first trident head-dress appeared over the hill to the east. They came in a long line, heading for the fire, a snake-marked spear in either hand. Bowing and backing up, they worshipped the fire four times from the east, then from the south, then the west, then the north and finally back to the east once more. The dance had many figures, one of which was a war.

After the night of dancing was over and the dawn was breaking, I made my way to where the dancers were washing off their black make-up. Selecting the main chanter, whose elaborate costume designated him as that of the non-dancing "governor" or "leader," I began to pull out some of the photographs which I had borrowed from the museums and with which I had fortified myself. First I pulled out some paintings of "Yama," the Tibetan ruler of Hell with his trident and red skull-cap whose scarlet fringe so reminds one of the crown of the Incas. As the word Yama in Japanese means "mountain," this is undoubtedly the old volcanic deity whom the present Buddhist religion, like the Christian, has consigned to the underworld.

The man to whom I had addressed myself waved me away with a "No-savvy" and partly turned his back, but some of the young men stepped up and took the pictures, commenting in Indian. He partly turned back, interested in spite of himself. I explained in English where this masked figure was from, pointing out the head dress of horns against a background of flames. For a while I had the feeling that I was talking to the air, for these mask-like faces gave no indication that I was being listened to or understood. They returned the pictures with nothing more than an amused shrug.

I then produced some photographs of temple paintings of Egypt. One brought startled comments in Indian and shouts to others to come and look. It was a temple-wall representation of Am-mon-Ra.

"What Indian tribe painted this picture?" asked the man who had just told me that he "no-savvied" the English language.

"That is a temple painting of Ancient Egypt. You can see for yourself the likeness to your fire-god in this fire-god and sun-god of the ancients. I would like to know if the names are similar. Would it be possible to tell me yours?"

"No, it would not," he answered not unkindly and then continued to explain, "You see, his name is strictly forbidden to ever mention aloud. We believe that to do so would bring bad luck and again when we want the power of that name it would be lacking to us."

"Then I shall tell you the name of the Egyptian god. If it is close, will you tell me?"

"I see no harm in allowing you to guess if you wish."

"The name of the Egyptian god is AMON-RA."

An audible gasp came from them all and they stared at each other in a most startled, even frightened, manner.

"The name is identical."

I was not prepared for this myself. Navaho informants had told me it was similar but, this was almost unbelievable! Amon-Ra under his Egyptian name!

"Your language is probably Asian," I found myself thinking aloud.

"Yes, so they tell us."

"Then since this is called the Devil Dance, you do not worship him but regard him as chief-of-devils?"

His lips straightened to a thin hard line.

"The name Devil Dance was given by enemies. This is The-Crown-Dance, and he is the mighty ruler of The-Men-of-the-Mountains. He is good, not bad. Only enemies say he is bad."

There was no doubt that the Apaches identified themselves with Amon-Ra and not against him, their Athapascan tongue notwithstanding.

"Could you tell me from which direction he came?"

"As you yourself saw tonight, he came with his Men-of-the Mountains from the east, out of the Fire-Land which was in the midst of the waters. He and his people then turned south where they built cities high on the crests of mountains and again worshipped the Sacred Fire."

If I had been listening to a typical Carib I might have expected these Caribbean traditions. I might not have been surprised from a Sioux or a member of the Iroquois or Muskogean groups. These were Carib traditions, but Caribs speaking Athapascan! Memories of conversations I had had with the Athapascan Chippewayans in the wild tundra of Canada flashed into my mind. They too remembered the fire-god of the south who came out of the sunrise sea when the world was young, but he was a powerful devil whom they had conquered! Then suddenly this last sentence began to register on my wandering mind.

"You turned south and built cities on the crests of mountains? Were they cities built of giant stones?"

"Yes, very large stones. In those days our people had the strength of the stars," he said, touching his breasts where two mirrors flashed, one on either breast.

"What do you mean by that?" I asked.

I noticed that the young men were beginning to look most embarrassed.

"I mean," he said, glancing at them slowly and defiantly, "that once we were People-of-The-Stars, and the Twin-Stars were on the horns of our crown."

Could this be Venus-Calendar? The ever-present Carib tradition again? I began to count the points across the top of his cap, a sort of skullcap. There were thirteen. Below it were eight and between them a strange horned and lightning-arrowed circle. The appendages on the circle were twelve. Apparently I was wrong, but I would pursue the subject to the point beyond doubt since my informant seemed willing.

"What stars do these mirrors represent?" I asked, pointing to his breasts.

"The Twin-Stars. Those of the dawn and of the twilight."

"Let us be specific. The Dawn Star and the Twilight Star cannot appear at the same time because they are the same star."

"Yes," he answered bitterly. "The young men who go to white man's school say they are one star, the planet Venus! To us of ancient traditions, they were Twins and were upon the horns of our crowns!"

"And the numbers sacred to them were eight and thirteen?" I continued, ignoring for the moment the evidence that I had apparently touched upon a subject which had been the cause of a bitter theological argument between two schools of Apache thought. All now turned their eyes upon me.

"Yes," the old man nodded. "Those are indeed the numbers sacred to the Twin Stars, but how could you know that?"

"They are the numbers of the Venus Calendar," I explained, and one young man asked wonderingly:

"A calendar?" while another said: "Please explain."

"Venus, whirling about the sun on an internal orbit, makes thirteen revolutions to eight turns of the earth. This is what is known as the Venus Calendar. Its ancient use in the Americas seems to have been very extensive."

"You are talking about exact observation of the stars, and of Venus in particular?" one of the young men persisted.

"Yes, of course."

"You are trying to tell us," the old man now asked in the same puzzled manner, but with a gleam of triumph in his eye that grew as he spoke, "that we once observed the stars long enough to form a calendar, a most elaborate calendar covering many years?"

"Apparently so. Yet this horned circle only has twelve appendages, so I may be wrong."

"You did not count correctly. The inner circle is thirteen. And if you notice the Men-of-the-Mountain have twenty-six pyramids about their bodies (painted decoration over one shoulder and under the other arm), that is, thirteen for each of the Twin-Stars. And again our most sacred number is 104 which is eight 13s."

"Then you do have the evidence of having had the Venus Calendar!"

"But such a long observation would suggest cities and our white teachers have spent fifty years trying to convince us that all our traditions are wrong and that we could not possibly have once had cities in the east and in the south!"

It was the old man's hour of triumph and I sensed it as I answered truthfully enough:

"No scientist would dare to make such a dogmatic statement. After all, those numbers have something to say for themselves."

And then again his last words recalled to mind the remark about the giant stones on the crests of the southern mountains, and into my mind flashed the picture of that great figure carved on the gateway of mysterious Tiahuanaco in the high Andes, that figure with its two swords held in either hand speaking from a right-angled mouth. I turned again to my list of pictures and hunted through the Andes section. Intensely watching his face, I handed it to him. He gasped, and all began talking at once in Indian. Then, turning to the four directions, he called out loudly. Apaches appeared from everywhere, running to join us. The picture was almost pulled to pieces in the eagerness of one group to get it from another. Turning to me, he announced with finality:

"That is the city of our traditions."

"Now wait a moment," I cautioned. "Not so fast. In the first place, how do you know?"

"The position of the two swords is up. That means friendship with limitation, of course. It is a proper figure for the gateway. Then they are held at right angles to the upper arm, thus forming with the head a trident. That is the secret sign of recognition. That is our city. And now, where is it?"

"Very far to the south. It is in the Andes and has been in ruins from long before Inca times."

But he scarcely heard me. To those who were coming he was waving the picture and shouting in a jumbled mass of Indian and English something about "white-man's school." To one young brave, who was not painted or dressed up for the dance, he said with a sort of fierce joy: "Tell that to your teachers!"

In spite of the language handicap, I too could feel the thrill of the moment as recognition lit one face after another. A people long orphaned seemed to be finding its roots. But first Egypt and now Tiahuanaco! Seemingly it was fantastic!

"The figure could have been an accident," I warned.

The old sage turned a sobered face toward me.

"You are entirely right. It could have been. I, too, like to get the facts straight. Let us confer further. Was this city in the high mountains?"

"Yes, but it was situated on a high lake. There were islands. . . ."

"The islands were the sacred places, of course. Did great caves run under the earth from this city?"

"Yes, there is a legend among the local Indians that the caves in that region held most of the real city and that very little of it was built above the ground."

"Our cities were built so. But there was one city right on the crest of a range."

"Machu Picchu! It, too, was built by the Megaliths, the great-stone-builders."

"But the food, that, too, should tell the story. Did they terrace the land?"

"Yes, from the snow to the base, through many climates."

"And here they grew many foods now lost? Bringing the water from the snow at the peaks?"

"Yes, through tunnels no longer known."

He could see my skepticism vanishing as I stared at him. Could it be that these were The Megaliths? These children of war who, outnumbered hundreds to one, had made such monkeys out of our soldiers for so long, and, before that, had terrorized the entire Indian population of the North American Southwest for centuries, or perhaps for millennia. Then, suddenly realizing the opportunity, I pleaded:

"Tell me of the Old Land, the Land in the East."

"When we speak of those times, white men laugh."

"I will not laugh. I ask because I wish to know. I wish to know of things beyond the power of our histories to teach."

For a moment he searched my face, and then he began, while blanketed figures with the red paint across their faces in the old horizontal marks of the Caribs crowded closely around us:

"We lived in The Old Red Fire Land long before the Flood when the gateway had a place where you lost yourself. . . ."

"A labyrinth?"

"Yes. It was the heart of the world then. All things were straightened out there like things are straightened out now in Washington. Many nations straightened things out there."

"It was a great capital?"

"A very powerful one. Ships lost themselves at the gates unless helped to find the way in. The land was not very wide but it had the highest mountains in the whole world. And below them in giant caves dwelt the fire-god whose name we must never speak."

"Yes, go on. You give a graphic picture of a great sea power whose main port must have had an impregnable entrance."

"First there were the Twin Stars and the power of them, which is the crescent symbol. The Navaho remembers them as Boss Sparkling-Star-Which-Lies-As-Two. There were Four-Mountains. Here we, The-Men-of-The-Mountains, had our beginnings and grew to our greatness. Later, the Four-Mountains lost strength and eight more were added, making the total Twelve-Mountains. I cannot explain what that might mean."

"Perhaps an invasion of a foreign power, a settling among you of the conquerors and a change of calendar to the lunar or the twelve months or moons."

I waited patiently for much talk in Indian to play itself out, and then, to keep from missing too much, and to again get the conversation into English, I asked: "Did you have a figure of a horned sheep (the Egyptian ram of Ammon-Ra) among your totems?"

"Yes, of course. The great horned Mountain-Sheep spoke in those days and drew its strength from the stars when it lived on the Old Red Fire-Land."

"And the dragon? I mean the giant monster which was long like a snake and plated like a lizard."

"You speak of the fire-god himself who sometimes took this form. Yes, he lived in vast underground caverns beneath the Old Red Fire-Land, and when he crawled through his caverns, the whole land shook like jelly. It was through his anger that the Old Land was destroyed. That happened when he left his caverns and came up through the mountains, raining fire and death upon fear-maddened throngs. . . ."

"Ah-Musem-Cab, whose name means the secret red of the earth, came out of The Underworld in order to close the eyes of the Thirteen Gods. . . ." I found myself saying aloud. Then I stopped in sudden embarrassment as I found many pairs of eyes fastened in astonishment upon me. "Oh, forgive me, I hadn't meant to interrupt you."

"What is that you speak?"

"An old Indian book, perhaps the oldest on earth, the Chilam Balaam. It survived the white-man's fires of destruction and still lives to tell us of the Old Land's destruction by volcanoes and then by flood. But please go on."

"I would know more of this book."

"But for the moment my memory has failed me. Someday I shall return and read it to you."

"With this promise you lift my heart. There is no more to tell now of the Old Fire-Land. The people grew afraid and they ran away. They came west from over the water and after they landed the oceans went away and we never saw them any more, we who in the days of our greatness ruled the oceans."

"What happened then?" I prodded as the silence threatened to lengthen indefinitely.

"We went south along the ridges of the high mountains where we built our cities of the great caves."

"Did you build them then or were they provinces of the Old Red Land?"

Apparently he regarded this as quibbling, for his answer was, "Isn't that

the same thing? They were our cities. We made them great. When enemies drove us out of them we left by the caverns and wandering through them in darkness for years, carried food plants with us, though we lost most of them...."

Another silence followed and when again he spoke, it was apparent to me that the tale of the migrations had been ended.

"In the old days the tale was more complete, but today the young men are no longer interested in what happened to the horned Mountain-Sheep and much is being forgotten. Their teachers have taught them to call these traditions 'fairy tales' fit only for children in kindergarten. I know that there must be meanings behind those which are first seen, for the ancients assured us on their most sacred oath that although they no longer knew some of the meanings, the facts told had once been true."

"You are quite right," I nodded, addressing myself mostly to the solemn-faced young men, "none of us know all the meanings which have been lost through countless millennia of war and pestilence and famine, but perhaps with study, and comparison, some of the ancient meanings can be recovered. To me these old stories are infinitely precious, to be more highly valued than the finest gold. These fragments of folk-memory can never be replaced once they are lost."

With a grateful smile the old chanter turned away, but with my voice I reached after him.

"Wait!" I called, "There is one more point, a rather important one." And as he came back through the lane of respectful youngsters, I added: "It has occurred to me that the city of Cuzco in the Andes is built in the shape of a condor with every street a feather, and that its ancient fort, Sachsahuaman, formed of earth's largest building blocks and undermined with a labyrinth where a man could hold back an army, seen from the air is the head of the condor. I have also remembered that 'Con' is the native Andes name for the fire-god, and that the condor was known to the Ancient Greeks as the Phoenix or the Fire-bird...."

"I would know more of this bird!"

"It has a reputed wing-spread of fourteen feet; kills an ox by stabbing its heart with its powerful beak and can swallow a sheep. It nests on the highest peaks of the Andes and sails easily in the teeth of the blizzard. It is also at home in the Caribbean sea...."

My words had plainly electrified them. They had started to talk among themselves but all hushed when the old chanter asked:

"Has this bird the habit of eating alone, and does it wear a ruff of white feathers about its neck?"

"Yes. Both Carib and Sioux medicine men have told me that one would always know a Carib tribe by the neck feathers of this bird which must be gathered from a living condor, and worn above the forehead, as such was the order of the fire-god to his children."

"This must be the Bird-of-the-Lightnings!"

"Why, yes, that is its South American name! And by the way, I wonder if this is not the Thunder-Bird of the North?"

"How do you know these things?"

"By comparative study of tribe with tribe," I answered, but I noted that the eye of every Apache had fastened itself to the top-knot of white feathers above the helmet the chanter wore, that cap upon which the thirteen and the eight pyramids enclosed the horned circle and the crescents. Only a bold question would succeed in getting the desired information I knew, so I stepped forward, pointing to his helmet.

"If those are the white feathers from the ruff of the living condor, the Bird-Of-The-Lightnings, then you are true Caribs in spite of the language."

"I cannot answer that question," he said. But I did not need his confirmation. Behind his back a half dozen young men were nodding vigorously.

I smiled my gratitude to them and added for his benefit: "It is also interesting to note that, whether you wear the correct feathers or not, the shape of your helmet rather strikingly resembles those worn today by the Indians of the High Andes."

But he was giving me his dismissal speech: "The sun is already high and my memory has failed me now on further details of the old days. When you come again with the book, we shall confer again about the times when the Men-Of-The-Mountains ruled the seas and wore the Twin-Stars on their Horns."

I walked for miles that day without realizing that I had gone but a few feet. At times smiles of contempt probably crossed my face, for I was thinking of how much allegorical history is being daily lost in our time because some snobbish educated fool, in the complacency of his or her well-ordered little mind, has taught the youth of the red men to laugh at these supposed "fairy tales" of their ancients.

But such thoughts were but the cobwebs in the shadowy palace of the past. Caribs! How did we come by the ancient names of Carib or Cariao? Could Braghine's suggestion be true that the K sound stood for people as it did in the Pueblos, Aztecan, Muskhogean and other languages where it has retained its root sound, and A. R. stood for Ammon-Ra, the Hidden One whose name is taboo? Was this the meaning of Aruak on the eastern shore of Columbia and the western shore of Africa with its equally significant Tuarak or Tuareg?

Caribs speaking on Athapascan tongue, but true sons of that long-headed hatchet-faced red warrior race! Caribs, who, like their brother tribes, relived in their weird rites their lost millennium* of greatness; who remembered past the history of all living and most dead nations, to a time when an Old Fire-Land ruled the oceans, and who, in this day of airplanes and movies, still worshipped AMMON-RA!

AUTHOR'S NOTE: Here is perhaps the most interesting article of my whole Series, "The Mystery of Apache Tradition," to be inserted after "The Totem of The Wolf."

I was probably lucky to get all this information immediately, being a stranger to the tribe, but apparently my luck was due to internal dissentions over the truth of the traditions.

As is usual, I am withholding all names of Indian informants. It might not matter in this case, but in many instances, the informant is ceremonially killed after the publication of forbidden information. At any rate, withholding the name of the informant, as might be easily understood under the circumstances, makes for better Indian friendships and more authentic information on future occasions.

I know far too much about Indians to hold the lives of these old sages lightly, as, I am afraid, a few writers and too many scientists do. When one is killed, it is science itself that is the loser. At the present moment, Dr. David Banks Rogers, the authority for early man on the Channel Islands of the California Coast, is mourning the death of one of the greatest sages among the red men, killed because of the carelessness of a fellow scientist.

The discovery of the information contained in this article was one of my keenest pleasures, and one I am passing on to the readers of "A. S." in the hope that many of them will receive the same sensation as I did when the Apaches lifted the veil of secrecy and interpreted some of the ceremonial meaning of their famous, but misnamed, "Devil Dance."

REFERENCES For Condor Totem among the Ancients see Potnanski, the Bolivian authority. The Pageant of So. Amer. Hist, by A. M. Peck (Longmans Green & Co., 1941). Peru, a Land of Contrasts by Millicent Todd (Little Brown, 1918). Braghine: The Shadow of Atlantis.

THE SEARCH FOR THE "PALE PROPHET" IN ANCIENT AMERICA

The author of this story is purported to be the Navaho Indian named below. He tells us this tribal secret of the Paiutes in appreciation for the story of the Navaho which appeared in the Spring 1948 issue of FATE magazine. But the style of the writing is unmistakably that of L. Taylor Hansen, who here hides behind an identity that is again male along with being a pseudonymous Native American. Pay attention to how the subject of flying saucers induces a cautious awe in the elder telling the story; he says it is unwise to be too curious about the phenomenon. He is also careful to sidestep the notion of total belief, calling the airships something stranger than he can comfortably deal with.

Tribal Memories Of The Flying Saucers
By OGA-MAKE

Most of you who read this are probably white men of a blood only a century or two out of Europe. You speak in your papers of the Flying Saucers or Mystery Ships as something new and strangely typical of the twentieth century. How could you but think otherwise? Yet if you had red skin, and were of a blood which had been born and bred of the land for untold thousands of years, you would know this is not true.

You would know that your ancestors, living in these mountains and upon these prairies for numberless generations, had seen these ships before and had passed down the story in the legends which are the unwritten history of your people. You do not believe? Well, after all, why should you? But knowing your scornful unbelief, the storytellers of my people have closed their lips in bitterness against the outward flow of this knowledge.

Yet, I have said to the storytellers this: now that the ships are being seen again, is it wise that we, the elder race, keep our knowledge to ourselves? Thus for me, an American Indian, some of the sages among my people have talked, and if you care to, I shall permit you to sit down with us and listen.

THE SEARCH FOR THE "PALE PROPHET" IN ANCIENT AMERICA

Let us say that it is dusk in that strange place which you, the white-man, calls "Death Valley." I have passed tobacco to the aged chief of the Paiutes, who sits across a tiny fire from me and sprinkles corn meal upon the flames...

The old chief looked like a wrinkled mummy as he sat there puffing upon his pipe. Yet his eyes were not those of the unseeing, but eyes which seemed to look back on long trails of time. His people had held the Inyo, Panamint and Death Valleys for untold centuries before the coming of the white-man. Now we sat in the valley which white-man named for "Death," but which the Paiute calls Tomesha - The Flaming Land. Here before me, as I faced eastward, the Funerals (mountains forming Death Valley's eastern wall) were wrapped in purple-blue blankets about their feet while their faces were painted in scarlet. Behind me, the Panamint rose like a mile-high wall, dark against the sinking sun.

The old Paiute smoked my tobacco for a long time before he reverently blew the smoke to the four directions. Finally he spoke.

"You ask me if we heard of the great silver airships in the days before white-man brought his wagon trains into the land?"

"Yes, grandfather, I come seeking knowledge." (Among all tribes of my people, grandfather is the term of greatest respect which one man can pay to another.)

"We, the Paiute Nation, have known of these ships for untold generations. We also believe that we know something of the people who fly them. They are called The Hav-musuvs."

"Who are the Hav-musuvs?"

"They are a people of the Panamint, and they are as ancient as Tomesha itself."

He smiled a little at my confusion.

"You do not understand? Of course not. You are not a Paiute. Then listen closely and I will lead you back along the trail of the dim past. When the world was young, and this valley which is now dry, parched desert, was a lush, hidden harbor of a blue water sea which stretched from half way up those mountains to the Gulf of California, it is said that the Hav-musuvs came here in huge rowing-ships. They found great caverns in the Panamint, and in them they built one of their cities. At that time California was the island which the Indians of that state told the Spanish it was, and which they marked so on their maps.

"Living in their hidden city, the Hav-musuvs ruled the sea with their fast-rowing ships, trading with faraway peoples and bringing strange goods to the great quays said still to exist in the caverns. Then, as untold centuries rolled past, the climate began to change. The water in the lake went down until there was no longer a way to the sea. First the way was broken only by the southern mountains, over the tops of which goods could be carried. But as time went by, the water continued to shrink, until the day came when only a dry crust was all that remained of the great blue lake. Then the desert came, and the Fire-God began to walk across Tomesha, The Flaming-Land.

"When the Hav-musuvs could no longer use their great rowing-ships, they began to think of other means to reach the world beyond. I suppose that is how it happened. We know that they began to use flying canoes. At first they were not large, these silvery ships with wings. They moved with a slight whirring sound, and a dipping movement, like an eagle. The passing centuries brought other changes. Tribe after tribe swept across the land, fighting to possess it for a while and passing like the storm of sand. In their mountain city still in the caverns, the Hav-musuvs dwelt in peace, far removed from the conflict. Sometimes they were seen in the distance, in their flying ships or riding on the snowy-white animals which took them from ledge to ledge up the cliffs. We have never seen these strange animals at any other place. To these people the passing centuries brought only larger and larger ships, moving always more silently."

"Have you ever seen a Hav-musuv?"

"No, but we have many stories of them. There are reasons why one does not become too curious."

"Reasons?"

"Yes. These strange people have weapons. One is a small tube which stuns one with a prickly feeling like a rain of cactus needles. One cannot move for hours, and during this time the mysterious ones vanish up the cliffs. The other weapon is deadly. It is a long, silvery tube. When this is pointed at you, death follows immediately."

"But tell me about these people. What do they look like and how do they dress?"

"They are a beautiful people. Their skin is a golden tint, and a head band holds back their long dark hair. They dress always in a white fine-spun garment which wraps around them and is draped upon one shoulder. Pale sandals are worn upon their feet...'

His voice trailed away in a puff of smoke. The purple shadows rising up the walls of the Funerals splashed like the waves of the ghost lake. The old man seemed to have fallen into a sort of trance, but I had one more question.

"Has any Paiute ever spoken to a Hav-musuv, or were the Paiutes here when the great rowing-ships first appeared?"

For some moments I wondered if he had heard me. Yet, as is our custom, I waited patiently for the answer. Again he went through the ritual of the smoke-breathing to the four directions, and then his soft voice continued:

THE SEARCH FOR THE "PALE PROPHET" IN ANCIENT AMERICA

"Yes. Once in the not-so-distant-past, but yet many generations before the coming of the Spanish, a Paiute chief lost his bride by sudden death. In his great and overwhelming grief, he thought of the Hav-musuvs and their long tube-of-death. He wished to join her, so he bid farewell to his sorrowing people and set off to find the Hav-musuvs. None appeared until the chief began to climb the almost un-scaleable Panamint. Then one of the men in white appeared suddenly before him with the long tube and motioned him back. The chief made signs that he wished to die, and came on. The man in white made a long singing whistle and other Hav-musuvs appeared. They spoke together in a strange tongue and then regarded the chief thoughtfully. Finally they made signs to him making him understand that they would take him with them.

"Many weeks after his people had mourned him for dead, the Paiute chief came back to his camp. He had been in the giant underground valley of the Hav-musuvs, he said, where white lights which burn night and day and never go out, or need any fuel, lit an ancient city of marble beauty. There he learned the language and the history of the mysterious people, giving them in turn the language and legends of the Paiutes. He said that he would have liked to remain there forever in the peace and beauty of their life, but they bade him return and use his new knowledge for his people."

I could not help but ask the inevitable: "Do you believe this story of the chief?"

His eyes studied the wisps of smoke for some minutes before he answered.

"I do not know. When a man is lost in Tomesha, and the Fire-God is walking across the salt crust, strange dreams, like clouds, fog through his mind. No man can breathe the hot breath of the Fire-God and long remain sane. Of course, the Paiutes have thought of this. No people knows the moods of Tomesha better than they.

"You asked me to tell you the legend of the flying ships. I have told you what the young men of the tribe do not know, for they no longer listen to the stories of the past. Now you ask me if I believe. I answer this. Turn around. Look behind you at that wall of the Panamint. How many giant caverns could open there, being hidden by the lights and shadows of the rocks? How many could open outward or inward and never be seen behind the arrow-like pinnacles before them? How many ships could swoop down like an eagle from the beyond, on summer nights when the fires of the furnace-sands have closed away the valley from the eyes of the white-man? How many Hav-musuvs could live in their eternal peace away from the noise of white-man's guns in their un-scaleable stronghold? This has always been a land of mystery. Nothing can change that. Not even white-man with his flying engines, for, should they come too close to the wall of the Panamint, a sharp wind like the flying arrow can sheer off a wing. Tomesha hides its secrets well even in winter, but no man can pry into them when the Fire-God draws the hot veil of his breath across the passes.

"I must still answer your question with my mind in doubt, for we speak of a weird land. White-man does not yet know it as well as the Paiutes, and we have ever held it in awe. It is still the forbidden 'Tomesha - Land-Of-The-Flaming-Earth.'"

Coincidentally or not, this same "legend" was repeated in amazing similarity by an old prospector by the name of Bourke Lee in his book "DEATH VALLEY MEN." (Macmillan Co., New York, 1932)

However, Lee stated that it was NOT a legend, but an actual account of the discovery of a (now abandoned) city WITHIN the Panamint Mountains as he heard it from three other people who claimed to have seen this ancient wonder beneath the earth.

THE SEARCH FOR THE "PALE PROPHET" IN ANCIENT AMERICA

THE SEARCH FOR THE "PALE PROPHET" IN ANCIENT AMERICA

This essay recounts the story of an epic battle between two powerful supernatural entities, among other fascinating bits of Native American lore. Hansen also wistfully fantasizes about a future anthropologist (again characterized as male, obligatory to the times) who would someday come along to verify the theories she could only sketch in briefly and incompletely. She is, however, the consummate anthropological professional herself, combining her own field work with decades of studying the available literature on the "Amerind," an old shorthand for American Indian.

Where Was The War Of The Wind God?
The legend of this symbolic war is one of the mysteries of the Indian folklore of the Americas.
By L. Taylor Hansen

When Quetzalcoatl began his trek of the Americas, he evidently found two great totems in religious conflict. One of these was that of the Wind-god and one was the Great Dragon. To the first, the element was that of the air, the weapon was that which flew through the air, namely the arrow tipped with feathers. The houses were circular. The Algonquin and the Eskimo both give the same reasons for their circular houses: they do not wish to trap the mighty breath of the Wind-god. The sacred totem animals were the king of birds upon one hand, and the most beautiful of birds on the other, namely, the Eagle and the Quetzal.

At this distance away from him, it is impossible to tell whether the Great White Reformer found a continent suffering from the results of a recent conflict, or whether he found an amalgamated totem which he took over for himself. For us the result is the same. We cannot tell at our distance whether or not Quetzalcoatl did the amalgamating. We cannot doubt that he did not wish to alienate either totem and wished to obtain converts from both. Or perhaps he had the amalgamated name thrust upon him by a people who thought in the terms of totems. Yet we cannot give him the credit for originating either, and most probably he was not the amalgamator.

What was the origin of these two totems, or perhaps we should say the direction from which the two entered upon the field of conflict? As is the way with Amerind legend, a single fragment makes almost no sense at all, but, in massive combination, many fragments begin to tell a story. And, as we go further along the way of Amerind lore, it is a story which is barely suggested. It is for future investigators to follow up the details. It is for the anthropologists of generations yet unborn, through thousands of hours of patient research, and years of living with half-tamed and unspoiled tribes, to fill in the lights and the shadows of the picture.

Yet that such a giant conflict did take place, perhaps long before the coming of Quetzalcoatl, and possibly not even upon the actual shores of these continents as they are today, seems an almost inevitable conclusion as we search through hundreds of legends. To begin with the Algonquin, let us recall the old Chippewa legend mentioned earlier, that millennia ago, before the flood, the Great-Serpent crawled out of the Sunrise-sea and fought the Thunderbird. At first it drove the Thunderbird west, but then the monster of the air came back and, after a conflict which shook the world, it triumphed over the Great-Water-Serpent.

The Choctaw and the Chickasaw, who speak the Muskhogean tongue, but whose language Gatschett and others believe is close to the conquered tongue of the Natchez, or that used by their serfs, have a legend that they came east following a leader with a pole. They were undoubtedly an amalgamated people for they claimed to be of the Serpent totem, painting snakes upon their cheeks and boasting to the early French that they had a cure for snakebite (as the Hopis have today), and yet they worshipped "Emeeshee," "The Breath-Master" or The Wind-God.

It is strange how this Wind-god holds his names. In this respect he is not far behind the Dragon, whose hundreds of names across thousands of miles cling to the original Amen or "Tu-Ajnen," although his worshippers speak languages which were probably mutually non-understandable at the dawn of history.

To the Papagoes, the Wind-god is "E-ee-toy," to the Aztecs he is "E-ee-catl," while the people of Jemez Pueblo tell us that he is the Elder Twin and his name is "Masee-we," which is not too far from "E-mee-she." The surprise is that working back from the Pueblos, whose mythology is much better preserved than other peoples both east and west of them, we find tribe after tribe falling into line that the Wind-God was the twin brother of The Wolf. Also, among the Aztecs, Tezcatlipoca, who is regarded as particularly of The Wolf, is the twin of their war-god who has many characteristics of their elder Wind-god, as distinguished from Quetzalcoatl, The Great

Reformer. They say that the first "Sun" was ended by a giant wind, the name of the day-star, in this case being used for an epoch of time. To these, one can collect hundreds of similar fragments, each adding the sum total of its weight that the reign of the Earth-monster was ended by a giant wind.

Among the Wallapai of Arizona and the Klamath of Oregon, the inverted pyramid means the wind, which is only another way of saying that the Wind-god defeated the pyramid-building Dragon. Nor should we forget that the Twin-god Myth is spread across the entire continent, now that we seem to be discovering the identity of the "Twins." The main thing which they did was to kill off the giant monsters who were devouring mankind.

The strange fact in this Twin-God vs. Great-Dragon War, (which should be carried out through the research upon the legends of every tribe, in order to be effective and to gain lost details, as well as to discard garbled ones) is that in the southern lands in those scripts which have survived the conflagration of the conquest, this resounding conflict and its termination is underscored. In "The Popul Vuh," for example, the fall of Votan's Xibalba, which revered the Earthquake-monster, Cabrakan, was caused by "Hu-ru-kan," "The Heart of Heaven." It is a curious trick of fate that the name of this deity should have carried over his old power into our English tongue.

Once more the Chilam Balam repeats the same story and again the Quiche Annals underwrite the triumph of the Wind-god. In the Quiche Annals, by the way, the leading god of the Quiches is Tohil, and it is rather surprising to come across him again in Central California in Kechai and Yokut mythology where he is the Great-Eagle, the most powerful being in their pantheon, under his ancient Quiche name. Linguistic comparisons between the Central American Quiches and these California groups are not available.

Possibly there is a connection of some kind between the Algonquin legend that the Elder-Twin, after the overthrow of the monsters, and the subsequent quarrel between the two brothers, was wounded by the Younger-Twin of the Wolf Totem, and fled east, the blood from his wound dripping upon his path and becoming chips of flint; and the fact that the Great-Bird of the Pueblo Sword-swallowing Clan has flint knives for feathers; as well as the fact that in the Aztec Calendar, the day-sign for The Eagle sometimes gives flint knives for crest-feathers. (T. T. Waterman noted the last of these similarities, and I am adding the former.)

Possibly, also, there is a connection between the black-and-white banding of the crest of The Eagle day-sign in the Aztec calendar and the natural black-and-white banding of the northern

Eagle war-bonnet. The symbolism of the war-bonnet, as explained to the present writer by a Sioux informant who wishes his name withheld, is that the circle of feathers represents the horizon, while the central red-tipped stalk rising from the center of the head of the wearer represents the sun. Is this circle of the horizon the reason for the circular symbolism of the Eagle Totem?

Other cultural-traits of the Wind-god when charted, as "The Sun-dance" was charted, may show an Algonquin center, though it must be admitted that the Oaxaca dances; those of the Otomi Indians in their "Flying-pole dance" at Pahuatlan, Mexico; and the pole-dance of the Ancient Chorotegans are among the uncharted members of this culture-trait, while the May-pole dance of early Europe may yet be proved to be a possible member.

Such cultural-traits are the circular home similar to the Algonquin "wigwam" and the Eskimo "igloo" and the circular "Great Dance Tent" with its central fire which is said to be "owned" by the men. In both the cases of the Algonquin and the Eskimo, the reason for the circular shape is given as the same. They do not wish to displease the Wind-god by making corners which might trap his mighty breath.

A similar trait is the circular sweat-bath which has a wide distribution, and, strangely enough, whether in California or in Michigan, is forbidden to women. Is this a sign, together with the fact that the men own the great circular dance house, that the Air totem of the Wind and Eagle was originally patriarchal? Or does it signify South-Sea-Island affinities? Perhaps we shall never know.

We do know that modern man was living in the Americas at a very early date. It is probable that when Neanderthal man was being driven from Europe toward Africa by disharmonic Cro-Magnon, the disharmonic Amerind was hunting the extinct buffalo (Bison Tayloris) upon the plains of Texas. If Wegener and his exponents of Continental-Drift are correct, and the Atlantic tear did not reach the North Polar Sea until the Pleistocene, then there may have been a land-bridge across the Sunken Appalachian Chain from Newfoundland to England over which man and mammal could have crossed during the long interglacial. If there was, much would be explained, not only the similarity in man's type, but the similarity in some cultural elements found on both sides of the North Atlantic.

The Wind-god bears internal evidence of being an ancient deity. Possibly in the first long glacial period, when, locked in the Americas, man saw the great mountains of ice creep upon his world in a relentless manner, he learned to pray to the waning sun as his only ally in a freezing planet. Perhaps this was the beginning of sun-worship, the Eagle-Totem, and the Wind which symbolized the breath of the sun.

It may have been this culture-complex which Cro-Magnon carried into northern Europe from the Americas where, during the first long glacial, he had consolidated his racial type. Yet if this is not the explanation, then there is much to account for in the early monuments, culture-traits and legends of the two lands.

Someday an anthropologist, perhaps not yet born, will take this absorbing subject for his doctorate thesis. He will trail the Elder Twin from the Pueblo of Jemez to the land of the Lapps. There he will note the babies in what we think of as Amerind cradle-boards. He will also note the cone-shaped great tent and mark the round sweat-house. He will be wiser than to claim with some that Longfellow copied the Finnish "Kale-vala" when he wrote "Hiawatha," merely giving it an American setting. Schoolcraft, the ethnologist, who first narrated these legends for science, wasn't recording Finnish tales. Nor could similar stories have reached western tribes in remote mountainous regions. Could Norse adventurers have carried home Amerind stories? It is possible but not probable. The only other explanation is that there was a basis for the tales in fact, in some Atlantic history that has long degenerated into legend on both shores.

This future ethnologist will note that Longfellow's meter is almost an echo of the pre-Aztec "Song of Quetzalcoatl," and he will no doubt record the fact that the Seneca, in gratitude to the poet and his recording of their epic "Hiawatha," which they declare he merely translated into English for them, for many years celebrated his birthday by an Amerind dance.

Our future student will follow the "Mounds" up to the coast of Newfoundland; note that the Eskimo of certain tribes claim a calendar which antedates their present climate in that it represents a warmer climate than they have at present; and then follow the "round towers" of Northern Europe across England to America where they trail out into the desert, and again pick up their path as they go on down to Central America. Doubtless, he will there note one which has a duplicate in Donegal, Ireland.

Without a doubt he will remember the Mediterranean legend of the slaying of the Dragon Tiamat by the god who threw the four winds into her mouth as she came up to swallow him. He will, of course, note the mischievousness of the Wolf and the striking similarity of his name across the Atlantic. He will, no doubt, touch upon Osiris. But as to whether or not he will be able to locate the site of this "earth-shaking" conflict when he writes his doctorate thesis upon this material, and doubtless much else besides, or whether he will be able to come to any conclusions, and if so, what they may be, is with the future.

REFERENCES

Schoolcraft, H. R.: Notes on the Iroquois; Indian Tribes of North America & Archives of Abor. Know. (3 Volumes).

Gatschett: Migration Legend of the Creeks from Brinton Library of Aboriginal' American Literature, Philadelphia.

E. C. Parsons: The Pueblo of Jemez.

THE SEARCH FOR THE "PALE PROPHET" IN ANCIENT AMERICA

The Ghost Dance of 1870 in South-Central California by A. H. Gayton, Univ. of Cal. Press (Amer. Arch, and Eth. Vol. 28).

The Mexican Indian Flying Pole Dance by Helga Larsen in The National Geographic Magazine, March 1937.

Schoolcraft-Longfellow-Hiawatha by Chase S. Osborn and S. Osborne Jacques Cattell Press, Lancaster, Penn.

Calendars of the Indians North of Mexico by Leona Cope (Am. Ach. and Eth. Vol. 16) Univ. of Calif. Press.

The Finnish Kalevala and some of the Early Irish Epics.

Wissler, C: Indians of V. S. (For accts. of Pleistocene Am. Man).

See Bancroft Native Races Vol. on Antiquities for details.

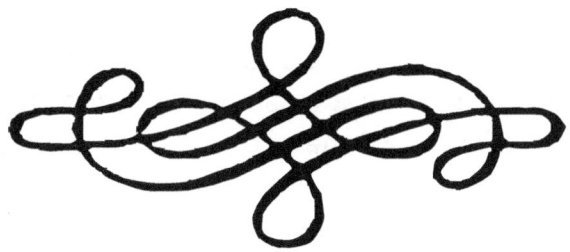

This is another essay that wonderfully ties together myths from various cultures throughout the world who logically should have had no contact or communication with one another. Hansen compares the Pacific tribes' veneration of the Great Fish with the Biblical story of Jonah being swallowed whole by a whale. The symbol of the trident, as associated with Neptune, the ancient Roman god of the sea, is also found here in the Americas. Hansen writes of Native American tribes who thought fish were too sacred to eat because some of their ancestors had been turned into fish. Once again, Hansen digs deeply into the universal ground of shared mythology and symbolism that spans the collective history of mankind and connects us all with some as-yet-unknown primal spiritual and cultural source.

Totem Of The Fish
By L. Taylor Hansen

One of the oldest totems in the world is that of the Great Fish. It is also the most baffling of mysteries.

The Pacific totem of the Great Fish is intriguing to the student of the ancient world mainly because of its antiquity. It is a totem which today has become almost completely submerged in later totems, but, in the early world, it may have been one of considerable migratory power.

Perhaps because of its antiquity, and its weakness among living tribes, who retain vestiges of it in a confused form only, The Great Fish is almost impossible to trace to a center. Therefore we shall discuss it as shattered fragments, possibly of an ancient entity, and possibly of merely accidental likenesses.

One of the earliest centers of The Great Fish is to be found among the prehistorical California Chumash who were centered upon the Channel Islands off the coast of Santa Barbara. The skeletons of these cemeteries were buried in the fetal position which a child has in its mother's womb. The graves were often arched over with the great rib bones of the whale. House platforms were arched by the same means.

Of the antiquity of the cemeteries upon the Santa Barbara coast there is little argument. Rogers, of the local museum, says: "At some time preceding the close of the Pleistocene (ice age) Period, there occurred a tremendous remodeling of the coastal region. Areas approximating in some places one hundred miles in width were suddenly swallowed by the sea, and, at the same time, a line of low-lying hills that had formerly straggled through the interior were now suddenly raised to a range of low mountains that bordered the new coastline. At the close of this movement, nothing remained of the fertile lowlands except a dozen or more islands."

Continuing the description of his archaeological work, on page 280 he says: "In a few sites, we note the devastation wrought by former earth movements, during which villages have been torn apart and sections of others hurled into the sea." Therefore, although he does not say so specifically, yet Rogers must date man's occupancy here to the Pleistocene, for he does say: "In the interim to the present time, the islands have been raised about forty feet. This movement has been slow and steady, for the beach line is without a sudden break."

This undoubted antiquity makes the Santa Cruz and other sites of particular interest, among the California Channel Islands.

Two animals seem to have been particularly revered by these people. One was the whale and the other was the dog. Skeletons of dogs, of two widely different domestic breeds, were found buried with great care and ceremony. One other curiosity was the fact that many twin children were found buried with the mother. This meant that to have twins was looked upon as a calamity and the necessary death of both, as well as that of the unfortunate mother, was to be expected for the good of the tribe. This same dislike for twins is to be found among some other coastal tribes, namely the Chinook. Were The Twins, the great heroes of almost all the Atlantic tribes, once enemies of The Great Fish Totem?

One other tribe which looks upon the birth of twins as a tribal calamity to be followed by the death penalty is a jungle tribe of The Amazon, The Waikanoes, who carry a decided Pacific culture. They claim "The Water Monster" for their totem. Their name for it, namely "Wai," is the Polynesian and Malayan word for water. Yet their "Wai" bears many marks of confusion with the Atlantic-Caribbean Dragon. Possibly this was due to the fact that the migrating Waikanoes found a Caribbean people before them, but the dislike of twins is entirely Pacific, as far as is now known.

Stanislaw Klimek, in his discussion of the structure of California Indian culture, finds the Chumash of the Santa Barbara region to be a rather distinct racial type which is distributed rather widely over California and is centered in the Yukian language of the North California coast, but is dominant over much of the coastal strip to the Santa Barbara region. He names the type "Paleoamerind" and describes it as having a long head, broad face, long trunk, short extremities and broad nose.

This is a good description of the Japanese and the Waikano of the South American jungles except that the latter is a round-head. There is a strong possibility, also, that length of limbs is not racial but due to feeding methods. It is a well-known fact that the sons and daughters of Japanese who have been born and brought up in America are all a head taller than their parents. And speaking of the Japanese, as well as the people of China, the Great Fish is much revered in their pantheon, although they are fish-eaters.

There are two other locations upon the mainland of the Americas where the Totem of the Great Fish has survived in a more or less mutilated form to the present. One is in the far north among the Eskimo peoples. They invoke the protection of the totem when they place whale bones sometimes above their summer dwellings and carve fetishes from the ribs of that mammal.

The other location is upon the Pacific side of South America. The totem apparently gained its main foothold upon the coast of Ecuador when that land ran much further out into the sea than at present. The crumbling of the western shoulder of the South American continent, which once must have taken in the Galapagos Islands, took place largely before the time of man. Yet that man was present when much of the now-drowned portions of the shelf was dry land is not to be denied. Relics, probably from cemeteries, are continually washing up upon the shore from unknown sites.

Julio Tello, head of the Lima Museum of Peru, and himself a full-blooded Qukhua (In-can) Indian, has done much work for science in this region. The mummies of priests, which he has removed from a certain archaeological site, are all preserved in a most interesting manner. They are mummified in a crouching or fetal position, wrapped with yards and yards of beautifully woven cloth, usually of a yellow or orange shade, and always adorned with fans. These graves were also often arched with whale rib. One immediately thinks of the fans of Japan and of China and of the yellow and orange shade which is so sacred to those lands. Did this have some lost connection, and if so, what could it have been?

Farther on down the coast was the great shrine of Pachacamac, which was located below the domain of intrusive Chan-Chan. This shrine, according to the Inca historians, was a very ancient oracle and a temple of healing. Here, in a massive edifice overlooking the sea, was the golden shrine of The Great Fish God. It was supposed to have been fabulously wealthy, as generations of rich princes had given presents to the ancient deity, while the entire surroundings were glittering with the most magnificent splendor. When the buccaneers of Pizzaro finally reached the shrine to tear from it the ancient gold and melt it into bars for Spain, they were greatly chagrined to find that it had been dumped into the sea. Thus the sea reclaimed again its own.

The only other site, which may have been touched by the long-submerged traits of this lost totem, and to which one must go in order to study it among living peoples, is among the Polynesians of the South Sea Islands. One is quite certain that here the power of the priesthood of the Great Fish is not dead.

It is interesting to learn that the old Polynesians believed that Tahiti and other islands rested upon the body of a giant fish, and that when they were shaken with earthquakes, the natives said that the great one was moving.

As one studies the totem, the biblical story of Jonah comes to mind. What could have been the significance of this myth, which undoubtedly was handed down to the Jews from the previous Mediterranean people? One cannot help but remember that the Atlantic Dragon is so often pictured as having swallowed a deity of some kind, or an ancient culture-hero, for a human face is so often shown looking out through the open jaws of the Dragon. Was this a trait which the Atlantic totem took over from the Great Fish of the Pacific? And was the later acceptance of the Dragon in the Pacific, and upon the mainland of Asia, made easy by the similarities to the anciently-revered Great Fish?

One other fact strengthens this possibility. In the ritualistic initiation ceremonies of certain Pacific Islands, the scars left upon the boy's body by the initiation knife of the secret society is said to be the place where the initiate was "swallowed by the Great Water Monster."

It might be very interesting if some archaeologist would undertake to map the American Indian into the fish-eaters and non-fish-eaters. Some tribes such as the Navaho and the Osage have such a taboo upon eating fish that they will not even accept candy in the form of a fish. And, similarly, from the Amazon jungles to the Mississippi, the fish-eaters invariably use a trident with which to spear fish when they catch them by this means, although fish traps and fish poison are as widely spread.

Usually, also, when asked the reason for these characteristics, the answer is the same. In the case of refusal to partake of fish, the informant always tells you that some of their ancestors were once turned into fish, which is simply the reason given for refraining to partake of one's totem. As for the trident spear, the answer is vaguer. Apparently the explorers never asked the Mississippi River Indians the reason, but, in the Amazon Jungles, the reason of the Tukanoes is that "it is the ancient weapon of the fish."

This answer immediately raises the long-sleeping memories of the picture of Neptune in our school mythologies, sitting upon a fish and holding up a trident spear. Did it have any connection to the great figure carved upon the monolith at

THE SEARCH FOR THE "PALE PROPHET" IN ANCIENT AMERICA

Tiahua-naco, Peru, which holds in each hand a trident spear? Or the Pueblo Indians who often carry tridents in their dances, or the Sioux who often cap their pyramid design with a trident?

Whether this was the weapon of the Great Fish, or of its ancient Atlantic enemy, we shall probably never know. Too many millennia have passed between us and the time when the trident had a mystical significance. And perhaps, like the Navaho, too many of the tribes have amalgamated again and again, keeping their mother's totem sacred without exactly knowing why, as they revere both the Great Dragon and the Wolf, although they remember that once the two fought for years, soaking the desert sands of the Southwest red with the blood of the battle.

One might as well ask the Nez Perce how they know that they remember when Mt. Hood threw a fiery rain, or ask the Tahoe Tribe, who from time immemorial have been hunters, how they know that they once had a huge empire of shining white cities which was conquered by a pyramid-building, fire-worshipping people? Or, when their island-empire was shaken by earthquakes after that conquest, and the earthquakes followed by the flooding of great tidal waves ever creeping higher, how they knew that they abandoned their conquerors who took refuge upon the central great pyramid, and, seizing the idle war-canoes of the conquerors, paddled away to safety? Ethnologists will tell you that the Tahoe Indians settled around their blue gem of a lake set among the high peaks of the Sierra Range because the hunting was good, and that they show not the faintest sign of ever having had the knowledge of a people who once built "white, shining cities." However, the Tahoe Indians will tell you, if you have sufficiently gained their confidence, that they settled upon Lake Tahoe because lakes are sacred, especially volcanic island-lakes, since those forgotten millennia ago when they, the people of the high mountains, were a maritime people of the sea. And who is to say that the ethnologists know, as yet, the entire story?

So it is with The Totem of the Great Fish, which is lost in the greater mystery of the Pacific itself, as The Totem of the Dragon is lost in the mystery of the Atlantic. Geologists are more or less certain that there could not have been an extensive land in the South Pacific during the time of man. That there may have been a far more extensive coral bench than the volcanic tops which the South Sea archipelagoes present today is probable. Gutenberg, of the California Institute of Technology, in his studies upon earthquake waves through the southern part of the world's greatest ocean, finds that they make certain patterns which definitely indicate the presence of some continental rocks, although undoubtedly long submerged. Yet, upon the other hand, Dr. Williams does not find as much possibility or subsidence in the South Seas as the eminent Darwin. (The latter scientist, by the way, has contributed as much toward scientific knowledge upon the subject of coral reefs as he did in the field of evolution.) However, Dr. Williams does find considerable evidence of faults and possibly of rift valleys in the tilt of the great volcanic caps which rise from the ocean floor, and which may be the remains of a gigantic system of oceanic Cordilleras.

Davis believes that Tahiti has been submerged some four hundred to five hundred feet by theoretically restoring the rock-bottomed valleys of what are apparently high range points. This is somewhat more than allowed by the return of the water to the oceans which was once locked up in the Pleistocene ice sheet.

What the story of these fragments may have been during the ice age, when they were apparently considerably larger than they were today, is hard to tell. If there was a great continental bench under them, it must have been submerged in warm, shallow water for the necessary millennia to become deeply coated with coral. Parts of this bench were then raised, probably during the general lowering of the sea-level due to the ice caps, thus causing the exposure of large coral islands. Through the coral of these beaches tore the lavas of the Pleistocene ice age. Today, with the return of the sea to the pre-ice level, and possibly some extra submergence as well, these lava tops of the old volcanoes are all that are left to tell the story. And we must read that story through their tilt to the sea and from the rounded coral pebbles buried in the flow of the Pleistocene lava.

What was the connection between the trident, The Great Fish, Jonah, Neptune and the early Oceanus, who was thought by the Greeks to have been connected with the name Maya? Or is the connection only an illusion caused by accidental similarities? Olson admits South Sea similarities among various Chumash pre-history sites, but believes them comparatively recent, and this definitely does not tie in with the antiquity of those at Ecuador. Even the Tahoe Indians, who from their legends are, apparently, a most ancient people, and who should know, do not seem to be able to help us out.

Thus the history of The Great Fish Totem; like the golden artifacts which today would be such an immense archaeological help, and which were reclaimed by the ocean from which they, or the ritualistic ideas behind them, might have come, sinks again into the greater mystery of the Pacific Ocean.

* * *

REFERENCES Tixiers Travels on the Osage Prairies. (Out of Print)

Chumash Prehistory by Ronald L. Olson (Amer. Archaeology and Ethn.) University of Calif. Press. Notes of the Later Geologic History of Tahiti by Howel Williams

Bulletin of Dept. of Geol. Sci. University of Calif. Press.

Tribal Initiations and Secret Societies by Edwin M. Loeb (Amer. Arch, and Etk.) University of Calif. Press

Rogers; Prehistoric Man on the Santa Barbara Coast

B. Gutenberg: Internal Constitution of the Earth. 1939.

Culture Element Distributions by Stanislaw Kumek, Univ. of Calif. Pub. Amer. Arch and Eth. Univ. of Calif. Press

Bancroft: Native Races. Vol. (Myths) 111. Davis, W. M. The Coral Reef Problem, Am. Geog. Soc, Spec. Pub. 1928.

THE SEARCH FOR THE "PALE PROPHET" IN ANCIENT AMERICA

Here Hansen has constructed an ingenious spider web of interconnecting words, making especially strong use of the recurrence of the word "Maya" (meaning the spirit of evil) from ancient India being found also among the indigenous peoples of the Americas, such as the Mayans. The details of the warfare of ancient peoples and their cultural intermingling is lost to history, but Hansen calls on the anthropologists and archeologists of her time to focus more on the Americas and help to answer the questions that so preoccupied her. Along the way, we hear about the orgiastic ritual dance of the dead monkeys, a tantalizingly spooky custom practiced in the jungles of Central America.

More Shadows Of Ancient India

Our own native America is inextricably linked with ancient India in a way that offers one of the great mysteries of mankind.

By L. Taylor Hansen

The Shadow of Ancient India hovers over the Americas in a most strange and persistent manner. One runs against it in the most unexpected times and places. Yet when one begins to search for it, like the shadow which it is, it becomes an evanescent thing and evaporates at a touch.

Of all the totems which might be traceable to India, that of the Monkey-god is the most surprising because even the names seem to coincide. Theodore Morde, of the Museum of the American Indian of New York City, and leader of the Third Honduran Expedition, writing in the American Weekly, tells of finding a lost "City of the Monkey-god" in the almost impassable jungles of Central America, Not only was he shown this ruined metropolis with its long avenue that led to the great idol of the Monkey-god, but he witnessed a feast of monkeys by the present occupants of the territory. These people considered the spider-monkey, which they called an "Uru," to be a particular delicacy.

In his article, Dr. Morde does not go into any details other than the barest outline of this strange and undeniably ritualistic orgy. He describes the gathering of the monkeys, and in particular the spider-monkey, which goes on for days. Then the dead monkeys are impaled on sticks which are placed in the ground so that they appear to be standing or sitting on a pole. A hot fire is built about the foot of these small poles, and, when the heat becomes sufficient, the muscles of the dead animals contract, causing them to dance with the most gruesome contortions in the light of the flames.

The student of Amerind lore, knowing that he is dealing here in the mainland nearest the Antilles with The Fire Totem, sees a whole historical sequence in this rite. "The Dance of the Dead Monkeys," as it is called, is certainly the triumph of the "Sacred-fire" over the previous totem. Yet this previous totem is not simply the monkey as such, but the spider-monkey, which is termed by the ancient name for the Spider Totem from the South Seas through the Andes of South America to the jungles, and from thence to our own Southwestern Zuni Pueblo. Is it possible that the Spider conquered a more ancient monkey-totem in Central America, amalgamating the two totems in the long-armed spider-monkey?

Dr. Morde suggests that these previous people may have been the Chorotegans. This is a particularly apt suggestion, since the Chorotegans showed many cultural similarities to Chan-Chan, such as the ritualistic beheading of females, while their metal work seems to be secondary to Chan-Chan, if indeed it is not the actual result of trade with that metropolis.

In some ways the Chorotegans seem to be a link between Chan-Chan and our Hopis. Both have beautiful polychrome pottery; both have similar styles for their women, and yet the Hopis, being matriarchal, seem to be the cultural children of a different totem than the patriarchal Spider. Could this previous totem have been that of the Monkey-god?

Dr. Morde is fascinated by the similarity of the totem of the Monkey-god with that of Ancient India. He recalls the story for the reader that Hanuman, the Monkey-god, an early deity of the Indian Ocean, carried Prince Rama and his beautiful wife Sita away in his bosom to safety when their land was attacked. Hanuman is pictured as a giant monkey. Rama, we will remember, a legendary emperor, along with his wife Sita, were considered to be the father and the mother of India.

Dr. Morde does not mention the fact that the Incas had a "Raymi" as well as a "Situa" festival, or that according to Guatemalan tradition, Father Xchmel, an early deity, had two sons by Xtmana (Itzmana?) who were known as Huncheran and Hanavan. Could the latter have been the Monkey-god Hanuman of India?

These India likenesses may, of course, be entirely accidental. They are so

THE SEARCH FOR THE "PALE PROPHET" IN ANCIENT AMERICA

few that they could in no way conflict with the Law of Averages. Yet there is another fact which may someday weigh the balance of the scales so heavily that they will tip toward connection. It cannot affect the situation today simply because of our ignorance of the subject. That fact is language.

We are still so ignorant of the relation of Amerind languages that we cannot, with any degree of certainty, compare the tongues of one hemisphere with the other, much less attempt a discussion of sources. However, Bancroft has noted a likeness of the California Pomo with that of the Ancient Malay. Taking, as a basis, one hundred and seventy common words, Bancroft finds that fifteen percent are Malay while the number that are similar to Chinese and Japanese are so few that they can be discarded as only accidental. (Bancroft, Native Races, Vol. 3.)

Some of the language studies done in the Pacific are most enlightening when compared with this list of Bancroft. Marsden, for example, taking thirty five of the simplest and most common Malayan words, finds that twenty will correspond to Polynesian generally, seven with a small portion of the dialects, and only seven remain peculiar to the Malay itself. Taking the same list which Marsden gave, the present writer found that almost all of them were identical with some dialect of the Philippines, while a smaller number were similar to some of the most archaic dialects of the Japanese. For example, Kali the Black goddess of Death has survived in Japanese as "koru" for black, and "ika" for fish in Malayan and Polynesian ("isda" in the Philippines and "iwa" in Java) has survived only as the name of a particular fish in Japan. Thus it is seen that Japan is much farther from the ancient Malayan than the Philippines. The Amerind tongues show about as much likeness as Japanese, though not the same survivals. Chinook and Paiute, for example, show a survival in the word for "sea" which also means "chief," and is repeated again on the South American coast near Ancient Chan-Chan. One has a suspicion that the entire substructure of the Pacific may have been ancient Malayan, but the lack of information upon the subject is abysmal.

Indeed the Malayan has entered the Mediterranean Aryan tongues in a small degree. The French "to eat" is a survival, as may be the Latin-derived English word "mangle" and Greek "manganon," war-machine of the Malayan "macan" ("maa" in Java, and "mangan," "caon," as well as "magan" in various dialects of the Phil.). In a similar manner, our name of "boar" for the hog seems to be a survival for this Malayan animal whose original name was close to "buai" (Chinese "buai," Japanese "buta," Polynesian "buaa" and "buai" in the Philippines). Or the English "battery," "battle" derived from the Latin "battalia" seems to be in turn derived from the Malayan "matte" (Polynesian same) which has survived in the Philippines under the more archaic (?) "bat-tai," meaning "to kill." Does not this seem to point to the early substructure of the Mediterranean also as Malayan, upon which the first Aryan invaders borrowed many of their words, and reared the later structures of Latin and Greek? Quantities of research must be done, of course, before we could be sure.

Sir William Jones, the distinguished orientalist, is of the opinion that the Aryan Sanskrit is the parent of both Malay and the Polynesian tongues, but Dr. Leyden, whose knowledge of the Pacific languages is perhaps more extensive than any other, denies this idea. He points out that there is no true Aryan in the South Seas. The Maori were cut off from Malayan sources before the advent of the Aryan and the words which Jones marked as Aryan are Malay-derived, borrowed by the Aryan conquerors.

It may be only an accidental fact that the early Malayans, who were described as brunettes with light-brown skin, which blended to a reddish hue, by the legends of India had black hair and eyes and were called Naga-Mayas. Yet the fact that their legendary emperor, Prince Maya, was known as "The Great Architect" is curiously reminiscent of Votan, who, we will remember, was of the Serpent Totem.

Prince Maya, according to some of the ancient stories, fled from the motherland which was being disrupted by volcanic convulsion and brought with him a famous work upon astronomy. Nor is this the point where the legendary likenesses between these people and Central America end. His people are supposed to have had animal totems.

According to the Ramayana (Hippolyte Fauche translation) the Mayas came to India from the direction of the sunrise and entered Burma, later spreading to India and from thence into the Mediterranean. In this connection, it is significant that the Egyptians are considered to have come from the east, and also that they carried the name "ra" for the sun, which is not only Malayan but also Polynesian and was borne to the outer circles of the Malayan language rings in various degrees of mutilation.

The Ramayana goes on to tell of the Mayas who later became known as the Dan-avas or the Pan-avas, a people born and bred of the sea, whose fleets penetrated every corner of the oceanic highways.

The Mahabharata is one of the great Epics of India which is usually considered to have been of Aryan origin. Like Homer's Iliad, it may have been, but its subject matter is reminiscent of the struggle between the races which took place during the millennium previous to its composition.

According to the Mahabharata, a huge conflict once took place between the Kurus, whose name is suspiciously like those for the Aryan Spider, and the Pan-Chatas. These latter were the five sons of Pan-du, explains the epic. If Pan-du was the Central-American and Mexican Pan-tu, could the Pan-Chatas have had a distant connection with the Pan-Chanes of Votan? Five of course, is one of the so-called "magical" numbers of the Venus-calendar. In the Mississippi Valley the

"Magical five" was continually symbolized by the Pentagon.

The main struggle, according to the Mahabharata, took place over the city of Hastinapur, which, it is explained, means the capital of the "ocean-dwellers." Where this legendary capital of the Naga Mayas may have been, we do not know, or in this case, to be more exact, the Pan-Chatas. Yet undoubtedly the Pan-Chatas were the Naga Mayas who were over-run so long ago by the "Urus" of the Kraken, or the Octopus-Spider with twelve legs, that today they are but a persistent legend, and, until the spade of archaeologists proves beyond a doubt the reverse, their science will continue to be thought of by the civilized world as having been the sudden and brilliant initial inventions of early Aryan India and Greece.

It is impossible to say, in the present state of our knowledge, whether there was ever any connection between these people and those of Central America who also called themselves "Mayas." We do not have the remotest proof as yet that these legends are anything other than interesting literature. Yet we do know that the name "Maya" is today, in the Brahman religion, The Spirit-of-Evil. That is in itself a significant fact. It gives science the strongest suspicions for believing that it formerly held a power which the incoming religion feared most desperately. Could it be only another coincidence that with Greek mythology, "Maya" was one of Ocean's daughters?

In the present "stage of our ignorance," it is idle to make any further speculations upon Peru, Central America and Pre-Aryan India. And until American universities stop underwriting Mediterranean excavation, and get busy upon India as well as the almost "dark continent," as far as archaeology goes, of ancient South America, we of our generation can only suspend our judgment.

REFERENCES

Morde: American Weekly, Sept. 22, 1940. The Languages and Literature of the Indo-Chinese Nation, 10th Volume of Dr. Ley dens Asiatic Researches, Marsdens Malayan Dictionary.

Bancroft: Native Races, Vol. Ill, Languages.

Lang: Migrations of the Polynesian Nation. The Ancient Bharata and the Ramayana of India.

Markham: The Ancient Incas.

THE SEARCH FOR THE "PALE PROPHET" IN ANCIENT AMERICA

Most of us remember the dire predictions made about December 21, 2012, based on a shaky interpretation of the Mayan calendar. The day came and went without much fanfare, as expected by most. But in this essay by Hansen, written many moons before the doomsayers special day, we learn about a way of counting time called the Venus Calendar, which has come down to us as part of the mathematical and astronomical genius of the Mayan people. The numbers involved are said to have originated in Pan, or Lemuria, a fabled location greatly esteemed by many with an interest in alternative or occult ancient history.

The Ghost Of The Venus Calendar
By L. Taylor Hansen

The mystery of the ancient continent of Pan, or Lemuria, may be inextricably entwined with this ancient calendar

Behind the most ancient nations stands the shadow of a lost motherland by the name of Pan, and in connection with that name, the sacred numbers eight and thirteen, with the amount of their difference, five. Over and over are these numbers repeated, until their very reiteration carries something haunting, so that one becomes, as it were, eight-thirteen conscious.

Then in these most ancient manuscripts, one notices a change, and the number combinations of and twelve triumph over the eight-thirteen. These numbers are usually spoken of as gods, but that does not in the least alter the significance of the change and the triumphing of the nine-twelve over the eight-thirteen.

Before one starts to study the calendar systems of the Ancient Mayas, these number combinations mean nothing, but after one becomes acquainted with the almost fantastic accuracy of Mayan mathematicians and astronomers, the eight-thirteen and nine-twelve combinations leap into prominence as keys with which, some day, the secrets of the past may be unlocked.

First, let us take up the 8-13. Venus, whirling on an inside orbit, makes thirteen revolutions about the sun to eight terrestrial revolutions. This is the basis for the Venus-sun calendar, possibly once used extensively by the Mayans, although in historical times, that is from the first century on, its use was probably only as a check-up on the other calendars.

Then as to the twelve. Most primitive people are aware of the seasons in a general way but they keep track of time by phases of the moon, as it is a shorter and more easily observable period. Thus the saying "Two or three moons ago." This is also true of tribes who have had more learning at one time, but who for military or economic reasons have reverted to the life of the forest-dweller. In this case, the learning is retained only by the priesthood, and if adversity should strike down the wise men before they have had the opportunity to pass on the knowledge, it degenerates into mere symbols which are considered to have once had some lost or magical meaning. Thus many who speak of so many years as so many "winters" ago still reverence the evening or morning star as a sort of god, and regard the numbers of eight-thirteen as having a magical power connected in an unknown manner with its presence.

As a tribe which begins with short lunar observations continues to prosper, and more complicated rituals, demanding a certain date for their observance, arise, such as those preceding the sowing of grain, the solar and therefore seasonal observation of the sun becomes more important. Yet as the people began with the observation of the moon, which by now is undoubtedly some kind of a deity, it becomes necessary to combine the lunations of earlier reckoning with the seasons. Thus arises the need for the lunar-sun calendar.

As the moon goes through twelve complete periods during one terrestrial revolution and there is a partial lunation left over, which will throw the lunar calendar of twelve months (or moons) out of line with the seasons, unless corrected, both our present calendar of months unequal in length, together with an extra day on leap year, and the Mayan Civil Calendar, are attempts to meet the solar discrepancy and retain the twelve lunations.

Besides these two calendars, however, the Mayans had also a purely lunar calendar which is described upon pages 51 to 58 of the Mayan Dresden Codex. It covers 45 lunations, or nearly 33 years. The lunar revolutions are arranged in series of five or six, the former at 148 days and the latter calculated at 177 or 178. These lunations, which are the necessary number between eclipses, form a cycle and are contained in the Tzolkin, This series is then re-entered nine times, thus forming a larger cycle of nearly three hundred years. Thus the lunar calendar of the nine cycles, which bears internal evidence of long observational periods, can be used as a check against the more primitive calendar of the twelve months, which is a sort of arbitrary affair. Twenty days, each with a name of its own, are concurrently run with a period of thirteen months. The Aztec calendar is similar to this. Probably they were taken from some form ancestral to both peoples. Yet it is characteristic of the Aztecs and their preoccupation with ritual that, having the samples before them of the mathematical and astronomical genius of the Mayan, they choose to ignore all precedent except this arbitrary and clumsy ritualistic calendar.

Discussing the Aztec calendar, T. T. Waterman wonders why the Aztecs should choose thirteen months when they might just as well have taken fourteen. He admits that the twenty days were chosen because twenty was the unit of their counting system. (This is, of course, the reason for the Mayan choice.) It seems to the present writer that the answer was given by Seler when he pointed out that the special reverence which the Aztecs undoubtedly had for thirteen was a survival from some sort of connection with the Venus Calendar. Furthermore, this is strengthened by the exhortation chronicled by Tezozomoc, which is referred to by Seler. The

Waterman attempt to refute Seler on page 315 of his treatise on the Aztec calendar is unsuccessful because Waterman speaks of the Aztecs as an entity utterly devoid of any connection with the more advanced Mayas who preceded them in time, and thus, culturally speaking, in the flowering periods of the two civilizations.

Therefore the question is not that which Waterman asks, of why should the Aztecs choose the number thirteen, but rather, why should the Mayans choose the number thirteen in their Ritualistic Calendar? Waterman admits that there were thirteen divisions of the Mayan armies, while the Aztec mythology has thirteen serpents and the thirteenth day was sacred. He does not admit the widespread regard for thirteen in Northern North America, nor the suspicions of scholars that there may have been Venus reckoning in South America. Nor does he mention the Mayan Venus Calendar. Therefore, although Waterman attempts a refutation of the Venus Calendar argument for the Aztecs, his weakness is the fact that he attempts to isolate the Aztecs, while no Amerind civilization can be isolated and, at the same time, be adequately comprehended.

The widespread use of the numbers eight or thirteen, or both in combination, among the tribes north of Mexico has not as yet been adequately studied. From a Tennessee Mound comes a shell disc which is undoubtedly of the Venus Calendar. A Hopi pattern, which is supposed to draw "magical power" from the evening star, is in possession of the author and distinctly shows the eight-thirteen combination. The Blackfeet have a ritualistic pipe on the stem of which a serpent turns around eight times, while above and below this symbol is a band upon which are thirteen circles,

The most intriguing of all is the combination carved deeply upon the rocks at Tule Lake, Modoc County, in California near the Oregon line. These petroglyphs had never been seen until the government drained the lake. They were as much a surprise to the Modoc Indians as they were to the white men. The Modoc have informed the author that in their tribal memories the place has always been a lake. Yet standing before this oft-repeated combination, sometimes with even rows of dots to one side, in three rows, 73 dots in all, divided once by a deep division cleft, one has the strange feeling of looking upon what are, as yet, some unreadable dates and possibly parts of an unreadable history. For again it is borne upon the spectator that the greatest common divisor of 365 (terrestrial) and 584 (Venus) is 73, and that the solar year is five times, the Venus year eight times and the combination (or "basic" period of Seler) is thirteen times this factor.

Perhaps the key to the past which this ancient calendar seems to hold will never even be studied enough to be inserted in the lock until you and I and our neighbor across the street get busy and faithfully copy the curious old "Indian petro-glyphs or picture-writing" nearest to our home before unthinking tourist vandals, who know no better, have chipped it away in order to carry it off for souvenirs. Yes, until we get busy and copy it faithfully at least once for one museum. If we have the real scholars' desire that the future may know, even though we may never know in our lifetime, we will copy it for several museums, sending one copy to each.

There has been up to now too much confusion in our thinking between the terms "ancient" and "primitive." The Venus-solar calendar is a perfect illustration, for though it may be the former it is certainly not the latter. Its complete computation took eons of astronomical observation and a most modern or sophisticated disregard for the shorter phases of the more brilliant moon. What people carried this astronomical masterpiece?

Perhaps, as in the way with archaeological questions, that one is related to many others. Why do we, in these days of better astronomical observation, still cling to a more awkward and primitive calendar? Why do we in all of our measurements cling to the number twelve, regarding thirteen as bad or evil'? Could the reason be that the number thirteen once carried connotations of power and grandeur, back in the mist of unrecorded history? Not our power and grandeur, of course, but that of an enemy power? Was the number thirteen, like certain gods of the laity, marked by our ancestors as "untouchables" before the dawn of our recorded history?

Possibly the hints of a previous Venus Calendar in Europe, the Mediterranean and Ada are incidental and entirely due to chance. Or possibly, if there ever was a Venus Calendar in the Old World, the evidence has long been drowned by the incoming lunar-solar and is now beyond recovery. Yet the slender links of evidence in the Americas are not beyond recapturing, and there is a possibility that their recovery by science may be the key that will someday unlock eons of long forgotten time.

THE SEARCH FOR THE "PALE PROPHET" IN ANCIENT AMERICA

THE SEARCH FOR THE "PALE PROPHET" IN ANCIENT AMERICA

THE SEARCH FOR THE "PALE PROPHET" IN ANCIENT AMERICA

THE SEARCH FOR THE "PALE PROPHET" IN ANCIENT AMERICA

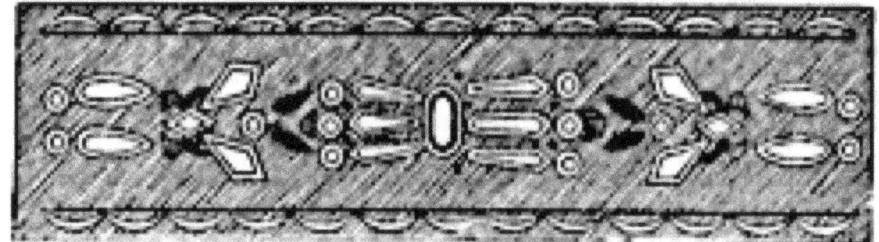

Sacred Evening Star Design of Hopis. (Owned by the author.)

THE SEARCH FOR THE "PALE PROPHET" IN ANCIENT AMERICA

The ocean-going canoes of the South Seas, which is said to have "passed from the eastern to the western oceans and from north to south, in ages so remote that the sun had not yet risen," may be part of the legend of Rama and Sita who flew in a great flying chariot, and of the "flight" of Hiawatha

Paper mulberry is used for bark cloth by the Mushongons of the Amazon, and is cultivated and used for the same purpose by the South Sea Islanders

The Naga of India, and the Huraha, bore names which mean "snake" and would seem to be derived from a common origin

The big question raised by these related facts is their origin in a —— motherland

130

THE SEARCH FOR THE "PALE PROPHET" IN ANCIENT AMERICA

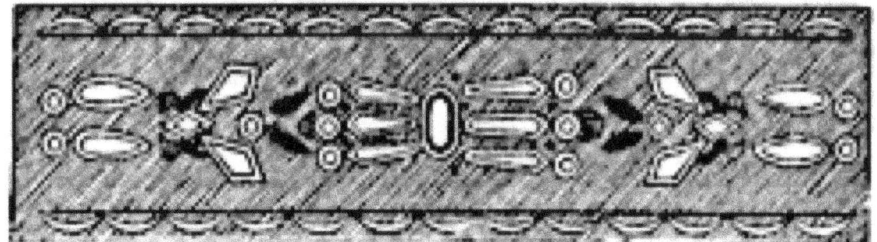

Sacred Evening Star Design of Hopis. (Owned by the author.)

THE SEARCH FOR THE "PALE PROPHET" IN ANCIENT AMERICA

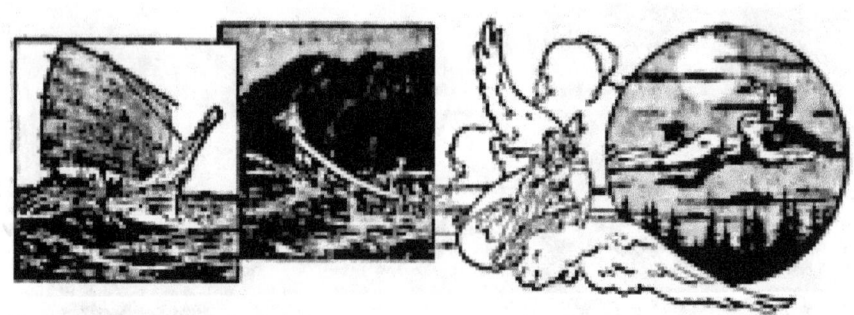

The ocean-going canoes of the South Seas, which is said to have "passed from the eastern to the western oceans and from north to south in ages so remote that the sun had not yet risen" may be part of the legend of Rama and Sita who flew in a great flying chariot, and of the "flight" of Hiawatha

The Naga of India, and the Navaho, have names which mean "snake" and would seem to be derived from a common origin

Paper mulberry is used for bark cloth by the Mundurucu of the Amazon, and is cultivated and used for the same purpose by the South Sea Islanders

The big question raised by these related facts is their origin in a ——— motherland

THE SEARCH FOR THE "PALE PROPHET" IN ANCIENT AMERICA

THE SEARCH FOR THE "PALE PROPHET" IN ANCIENT AMERICA

It is significant to note that the American Apache Indian is of the Totem Of The Wolf. The Apache are the prize fighting men among warlike Indians, and all had reason to fear them. Was it because they belonged to the Wolf Totem tribes? Can the Apache Indians have any real relation to the fighting Egyptians who are also of the Wolf Totem? Perhaps right here in America exists one of the significant anthropology clues

The American Indian legends of the Twins, the Elder, the Wind deity and the Younger Wolf spill over into the legends of Egypt in a very strange manner. There is a positive relationship which cannot be denied, and which positively indicates their common origin

The Dene people were apparently the last language to cross the Aleutians from Asia. Their tongue is so homogenous that it may have come as late as fifteen hundred years ago. In spite of this, their relationship to the early Dragon is most unmistakable

The volcano-worshipping religion might have been spread by lava outpourings on the coast. Or it is true that the legend of the Coyote who stole the sacred fire is the real basis for such worship. If so, we have a new link with the past

THE SEARCH FOR THE "PALE PROPHET" IN ANCIENT AMERICA

GEORGE HUNT WILLIAMSON came to realize that in America if you try to buck the status quo or change the system you can easily be slandered and identified as a dangerous dissident whether it be a communist, a fascist, or a neo Nazi. Many of the UFO contactees of the early days of the UFO/New Age movement were thusly labeled.

Williamson – aka Brother Philip – was at the forefront of those the government was keeping an eagle eye on for fear the Russians might be using him as a highly sophisticated mind managed and manipulated "Mind Soldier." *TRAVELING THE PATH BACK TO THE ROAD IN THE SKY* includes the entire text of Williamson's most accredited work linking ancient civilizations with the remote beginnings of humanity and visitations from outer space.

In addition, a vast update on Williamson's conflicted personality and his FBI papers has been added to this volume, as well as a fascinating commentary by Brad Steiger, who was to meet with Williamson to receive some important information when "Brother Philip passed away unexpectedly." —

J. EDGAR HOOVER'S MEN IDENTIFIED GEORGE HUNT WILLIAMSON AS A COMMUNIST OR AT PARAMOUNT A "MIND CONTROLLED SOLDIER" OF THE SOVIET UNION. . . OTHER UFO CONTACTS FROM THE EARLY UFO ERA WERE SIMILARLY LABELED!

THE SEARCH FOR THE "PALE PROPHET" IN ANCIENT AMERICA

Scientists tell us that the Hollow Earth Theory is bogus, that it's impossible that an entire civilization might exist below our feet which we know absolutely nothing about. Many claim that an advanced "Super Race" of humans have hidden themselves from the prying eyes of surface dwellers, and can only be reached by traveling to remote areas of the earth such as the North and South Poles and the expansive unexplored jungles of the Amazon where there are closely guarded entrances to this "Paradise" inside the Earth. Even the great explorer Admiral Richard E. Byrd claims to have traveled inside the planet where he was greeted by a fleet of flying saucers and a lost battalion of Nazi scientists. Here are 5 great books for your Conspiracy library.

DOES A VAST SYSTEM OF CAVERNS EXIST IN THE INTERIOR OF THE EARTH — AND HAS A "SUPER RACE" OF GIANTS HIDDEN THEMSELVES INSIDE A HOLLOW PLANET IN ORDER TO KEEP AWAY FROM THE PRYING EYES OF SURFACE DWELLERS? ADMIRAL RICHARD BYRD VISITED SUCH A "PARADISE," BUT HIS DISCOVERY REMAINS A CLOSELY GUARDED SECRET

www.ingramcontent.com/pod-product-compliance
Lightning Source LLC
Chambersburg PA
CBHW080513110426
42742CB00017B/3098